THE WRITE CALLING

Encouragement for the Writer's Heart

Endorsements

If God has called you to a writing ministry, you need this book of uplifting devotionals. It's written by writers—for writers. Do you ever doubt your skills, play the comparison game, get discouraged, or feel like quitting? Don't miss these encouraging words from nine Christian authors who honestly share their doubts, challenges, wisdom, and valuable advice. You'll find Scripture throughout these pages that will renew your passion for writing and remind you of why you said Yes when God nudged you to write.

—**Carol Kent**, Executive Director of Speak Up Ministries, Speaker and Author, *Speak Up with Confidence* (NavPress)

Every writer can relate to the sting of discouragement. The anointed authors of *The Write Calling* offer a balm to our aching hearts. As a therapist and fellow author, I recommend their encouraging words as a prescriptive aid to renew those called to write.

—**Tina Yeager**, award-winning author, speaker, podcast host *Flourish-Meant*, life coach

Writers need encouragement because we spend much time alone with our computer. It is easy to allow negative self-talk to take over. That's why I recommend *The Write Calling*. The authors are serious about the craft of writing, and they are full of advice and reassurance to whisk away the doubts. For all those procrastinators and perfectionists who need to remember their calling—get this book.

—**Karen Porter**, writing and speaking coach, author of *If You Give A Girl A Giant*, www.karenporter.com

This book is unique! All authors want you to read their writing, these authors want you to write as a result of your reading. This honest collection describes the ups

and downs of writing to inspire us in our own pursuit of creativity. Using the greatest Book ever written, we join them on their journeys of discovery of eternal truths. Read and enjoy! But more, read and let God release in you the desire to tell your own story, joining with the stories in this book, sharing with others in the Greatest Story ever told!
—**Stephen Gaukroger,** https://www.clariontrust.org.uk/

The Write Calling is a support group in book form. Packed with encouragement, it offers insights gleaned only through struggles. Through Scripture, stories from their lives, and suggested next steps contributors reveal the inner workings of every Christian writer's life. You'll nod your head in agreement as they share their doubts, comparisons, and questions, along with stories of joy, victory, and fulfillment—all designed to encourage you to keep writing. Whether you're a budding or established Christian writer, you'll find humor, truth, and hope in *The Write Calling*.
—**Patricia Durgin**, https://marketersonamission.com/

Let's be honest ... writing, while incredibly fulfilling and wonderful, can also bring frustration and loneliness. If you have ever put pen to paper or fingers to keyboard, you know the emotions of the writing journey. What if you had a mentor, a friend, who was further along on the path who could speak the language of all those emotions and understand firsthand what the writing journey entails? Now you do. In *The Write Calling: Encouragement for the Writer's Heart*, the authors offer blessed encouragement and understanding of the ups and downs of the writing life. If you are a writer, whether seasoned or a first timer, you will find this book to be a true treasure for your writing career.
—**Leah Adams**, Author, Speaker, Ambassador for Compassion International. LeahAdams.org

The Write Calling shows how writing is a gift as much as a ministry. Learn from these women, how they mastered hanging on when they wanted to let go— and how they accepted letting go of what bogged their writing down. A great addition to an author's library.
—**Robin Luftig**, Author and Speaker. robinluftig.com/

The Write Calling is full of sweet, poignant stories that pinpoint the fears we have as writers and provide direction on how to overcome them. These nine women vulnerably share from their experiences, and I found myself chuckling and nodding along as I relived some of the same experiences. Grab a coffee and your journal when you curl up with this book. I guarantee you'll have trouble putting it down.
—**Bethany Jett,** multi-award-winning author who is blessed to have been called to write. bethany@bethanyjett.com

The loneliness of writing is one threat Satan uses to shut us down. The encouraging beauty of *The Write Calling* is the diversity of her authors and their promise of companionship. As I read their writing and speaking experiences laced with, you can do this, don't give up, stay the course, I've been where you are—I felt included. Recognized. Validated. The authors provide priceless equipping based on personal experience from a professional perspective. *The Write Calling* is the right book to ward off spiritual heart attacks.
—**Linda Goldfarb:** Award-winning Author, Board-certified Christian Life Coach, and Award-winning Host of the *Your Best Writing* Lifepodcast.LindaGoldfarb.com

Writing is transformative. The words on paper have potential to transform the reader, but the process always transforms the writer. In *The Write Calling*, a collective of writing friends explore craft and calling, faith and fear, trials and truth encountered when connecting with others through the written word. In these pages, this writers group invites you to discover the personal growth you experience when you invest yourself in the worthy team sport of writing.

—**PeggySue Wells** is the bestselling author of thirty books including *Chasing Sunrise, The Ten Best Decisions A Single Mom Can Make,* and *The Patent.*

The writing life includes challenges, hard work, disappointment, perseverance, highs, and lows. *The Write Calling* provides practical encouragement for writers in all stages. Knowing someone else has been where you are helps. Having their support to keep you going is gold.

—**Debbie W. Wilson,** Bible teacher and author of *Little Women, Big God* and *Little Faith, Big God*

Many people have the mistaken impression that writers live a glamorous life, when, in fact, writing is often filled with challenges. From rejection and self-doubt to balancing writing isolation with family, writers walk an emotional tightrope. *The Write Calling: Encouragement for the Writer's Heart* honestly acknowledges writers' struggles but goes a step beyond with words of inspiration, encouragement, and practical advice. No matter where you are in your writing journey, *The Write Calling* is a book that will propel you forward.

—**Candy Arrington**, blogger, and author of *Life on Pause: Learning to Wait Well*

As a friend and family member of several authors, I know how important it is for writers to practice self-care. A devotional book, specifically for them, is important and much needed. The Write Calling perfectly fits the bill.

—**Rhonda DeSpain**, Business Owner

The Write Calling is a devotional gem filled with nuggets of spiritual truth bound to encourage and equip the soul of every writer to faithfully pursue their calling.

—**Kelly Goshorn**, award-winning author of A Love Restored

No writer should ever feel alone. And with *The Write Calling* you won't ever have to. Upon reading the honest stories, encouraging words, and practical helps of these authors, you will feel you are among friends, and you'll be inspired to keep writing, writing better, and writing for the One. Every writer, no matter where she is on her journey, should own a copy of this book.

—**Cindi McMenamin**, Writing Coach, Editor, and Author of seventeen books from Harvest House Publishers, including *When Women Walk Alone*

The writer's journey to publication—and beyond—is seldom an easy one. How does one go from raw talent to able wordsmith? How can we navigate the sometimes-overwhelming world of agents, editors, and publishers? How do we persevere in the face of rejection, self-doubt, naysayers, and writer's block? Thankfully, a group of seasoned writers, The Women of Living Write Texas, has compiled a beautiful collection of essays offering practical advice as well as emotional and spiritual encouragement for aspiring writers. If you are at the beginning of your writing journey, be sure to carry *The Write Calling* with you. It will undoubtedly help you every step of the way.

—**Ann Tatlock**, award-winning novelist, editor, and writing coach

If you call yourself a writer or have been called to write, you must read *The Write Calling: Encouragement for the Writer's Heart*. This collaboration of essays will assuage

your fears, inspire your words, and give you the tips and tools to produce your best work. Contributors are honest about their own battles with writing and willingly share the secrets to overcoming mindsets and weaknesses that keep your work from being seen, published, and read. If you're a writer or you know one, get this book today!
—**Robyn Dykstra**, National Christian Speaker, Best Selling Author, Professional Speaker Coach

These short messages uniquely for writers pack a big punch. As writers, how greatly we need these gentle encouragements, strong challenges, and timeless reminders! They steady us on the path God has given us to use words for his glory. Eloquent and astute, yet so like a friend across the kitchen table, the devotional writings from *The Write Calling: Encouragement for the Writer's Heart* is like a multi-vitamin for every writer.
—**Kyle Hunter**, Author of *Prodigals in Provence*

The Write Calling may have been written to empower and equip writers, but you don't have to be a writer to find the gems in this treasure chest of wisdom. They are encouraging, yet authentic in sharing the struggles and provide some practical points to overcome the many obstacles. If you have any desire to do something for God's kingdom, there is valuable information that will challenge you to go to another level.
—**Lisa Granger**, Host of A Woman's Heart on FM93.5 WMBG radio, podcaster

The Write Calling, Encouragement for the Writer's Heart uses three words any author would appreciate—calling, encouragement, and heart. This book is thought producing and caring—written just for writers. Each chapter touches the heart and soul in different ways. I recommend this book for those who spend hours putting pen to pad and using their mind and heart to communicate to others.

—**Robin Rohrback**, Human Resources Professional

THE WRITE CALLING

Encouragement for the Writer's Heart

THE WOMEN OF LIVING WRITE TEXAS

ELK LAKE PUBLISHING INC

PUBLISHING THE POSITIVE
Plymouth, Massachusetts

COPYRIGHT NOTICE

Cover and Interior Design:
Editor(s): Pam Lagomarsino, Deb Haggerty

PUBLISHED BY: Elk Lake Publishing, Inc., 35 Dogwood Drive, Plymouth, MA 02360, 2022

Library Cataloging Data

Names: DeArmond, Deb (Deb DeArmond)

The Write Calling: Encouragement for the Writer's Heart Deb DeArmond

212 p. 23cm × 15cm (9in × 6 in.)

ISBN-13: 978-1-64949-587-7 (paperback) | 978-1-64949-588-4 (trade paperback) | 978-1-64949-589-1 (e-book)

Key Words: Inspiration for Christian Writers; Encouragement for aspiring writers; Supporting the discouraged writer; Motivational moments for Christian writers; craft of writing; authors; writers

Library of Congress Control Number: 2022938987 Nonfiction

DEDICATION

To every writer who wonders, "when is it my turn, Lord?"

Never forget—those who write to fulfill God's call are ministering to the lives they touch—whether they blog, write novels, or nonfiction.

Stay the course. Someone is waiting for the words God has placed in your heart.

And the desire to move from writer to author burns bright.

TABLE OF CONTENTS

INTRODUCTION
AM I A WRITER?

Lori Altebaumer

The master said, 'Well done, my good and faithful servant. You have been faithful in handling this small amount, so now I will give you many more responsibilities.

—Matthew 25:23 NLT

Definition of a writer ... someone who writes.

What? You were expecting something more insightful and erudite? I'm a writer, not a semanticist.

So ... sorry, but if you put pen to paper or fingers to the keyboard to capture thoughts and ideas on paper, you, my friend, are a writer. That's all ... the single requirement you need to claim the coveted title of Writer.

There are no criteria to specify what education level you must attain, what your sales numbers should be, or how many awards hang on your office walls.

If you want to pursue a profession offering board certification to prove you are what you say you are, you'll need to consider becoming a doctor or lawyer. Unlike many occupations, a brain surgeon, for example, there is no minimum competency level you must achieve to be a writer. Life might be easier if there were.

Owning the title of writer like we believed the designation to be true would be more comfortable if there were a test to pass—an official certification board to approve my status as a writer. Then maybe I'd feel official. In the words of the Velveteen Rabbit, "I am real. I am real. The boy said so."[1]

(Of course, I should also note the Skin Horse cautioned the Velveteen Rabbit with, "Generally, by the time you are real, most of your hair has been loved off, and your eyes drop out and you get loose in the joints and very shabby.")[2]

It is a disturbing truth that one of the most powerful professions in the world has no other criteria to claim the role other than the physical act of our presence at the keyboard.

But I warn you, there is a vast difference between being a writer and being read.

Perhaps I'm being dramatic or sentimental about life as a writer, but the gift is an honor I take in all seriousness. Since I first learned to read, I've held in high esteem those who can capture the imagination and move the heart with words on paper. This is a gift not to take for granted—a sacred honor requiring our faithful stewardship.

Like the story of the master's talents from the gospel of Matthew, we have been given something of value which bears a responsibility (see Matthew 25:20–30). We've been entrusted with an idea—the seed of a message we must tend with care. We've been blessed with the freedom to capture our thoughts on paper. Maybe we've received the gift of time or financial support. The "talents" might look different, but none of them are any less valuable because of their variety.

But there is one more thing we need to steward well when we seek to be called a writer.

Too many who call themselves writers, while correct in the strictest of definitions, have failed to realize unless they crucify their writing on the cross of self, the work will never carry out the intended purpose.

There is a saying to write is to pour oneself out on the page. If we want our words to be deep and meaningful, this is a truth we must accept and live by. Our writing is emptied of us and filled with Jesus through the honest pouring out of ourselves onto paper.

This may be the board examination, the litmus test of truth, the gauntlet we accept if we want to be known as writers.

And we can do this hard work, this painful part of calling ourselves writers, with the knowledge, in the end, we will hear, "Well done, my good and faithful servant."

NEXT STEPS:

Read Matthew 25:14–30. Consider what in your life you can equate to the talents the master entrusted to the servants. Is now your time? Your passion for a certain message? Your creativity in telling a story? Your sense of humor in tearing down walls? Your love of exploration? Make your list as thorough as possible, including supporting family members and encouraging friends, the opportunity for a mentor … everything that makes your pursuit of this calling possible.

Now consider how you are stewarding these talents. What do you need to add, abandon, or change so you will hear "well done, my good and faithful servant"?

INSPIRATION IS ALL AROUND YOU

LESLIE THOMPSON

For his invisible attributes, namely, his eternal power
and divine nature, have been clearly perceived, ever
since the creation of the world, in the things that
have been made.

—Romans 1:20 ESV

Sometimes the creative process comes easy. We wake
up inspired and eager to dive into our current project. We
get caught up in our work and feel like time stands still as
words flow without effort onto the page. Other times, we
feel stuck, frustrated, or uninspired. We're trudging through
the wilderness, looking for an oasis of inspiration, but the
waters have run dry. What do you do when you feel defeated
because your creativity is parched? How do you overcome
a slump and reawaken the joy that keeps you motivated?

We are made in the image of our Creator, which means
God made us with the ability and unction to create. Although
we cannot manifest material from the void of the cosmos,
like God the Father, we can look to that which exists to
reignite our creative spark. As we marvel at both the
intricate details and vast expanse of God's workmanship,
we soon find our imagination springs back to life.

Many years ago, I took my husband on vacation to
Puerto Rico for his fiftieth birthday. I saved money for more

than a year and made clandestine arrangements for one of his best friends to meet us on the island as a surprise. Our friend was a master scuba diver, and I had signed us up for lessons, so we could join him in exploring the corals and sea life deep underwater.

Unfortunately, I swallowed a good bit of the ocean on our first day out and felt pretty puny that evening. I decided to recuperate the next day rather than continue the lesson. I hoped to rejoin the guys later. But I packed my laptop and perched underneath a shade tree on the beach, so I could watch my husband out in the water and congratulate him when they took a break for lunch.

I'm not sure I have ever been more productive as a writer than during those few hours on that secluded shoreline. The warm breeze, smell of the ocean, and playful squawks of seagulls overhead dazzled my senses. As I worked on a series of articles for a corporate client, my toes nestled in the sand, writing felt effortless. I was so enraptured by my surroundings, and though I tackled less stimulating subject matter in my work, I felt pure joy.

> And God said, "Let the earth sprout vegetation, plants yielding seed, and fruit trees bearing fruit in which is their seed, each according to its kind, on the earth." And it was so. The earth brought forth vegetation, plants yielding seed according to their own kinds, and trees bearing fruit in which is their seed, each according to its kind. And God saw that it was good.
>
> —Genesis 1:11-12 ESV

Back in our suburban subdivision, I still find connecting with nature gives me creative energy. Sometimes, the simple choice to stand up from my desk and take ten minutes to water plants in the backyard is all I need to get a second wind. Other times, I will walk at a nearby park or book a weekend at a cabin in the woods to get away from the world's distractions. When I lived in a cramped Manhattan apartment, I used to buy myself a bouquet of tulips from the bodega down the street. Having colorful flowers on my desk made my heart smile and often gave me enough of a creative nudge to push past mental blocks.

A writer friend loves to go fishing or sit by the fire pit and look at the stars to replenish the well of her imagination. When she isn't working on a particular project, she still seeks opportunities to put away electronic devices and connect with the organic world around her to nurture her soul.

When you need fresh ideas or renewed vision to move your writing projects forward, remember God created heaven and earth and everything in them. Look to his handiwork for inspiration, and partner with the one who gave you a unique message and talent to put your gifts to use for his glory.

Next Steps:

If you're having a hard time getting in a creative gear, put your project in park and refuel. Take a walk, pick a flower, listen to the birds, or pet a cat. Whether for an hour or a week, take time to soak up the beauty and wonder of nature, and soon you'll be ready to roll!

HUMBLE PIE DOES A BODY GOOD!

DEB DEARMOND

Without counsel plans fail, but with many advisers they succeed.

—Proverbs 15:22 ESV

"Absolutely not! *I can't change this paragraph.* God gave me this book and the words to write, so I declined the edits. *Changing this would be a sin!*"

As a writing coach, I've heard this—or something similar—several times. I wonder why the aspiring author works with a coach if they believe the text is from God's lips to their ears.

If we could all receive the same download as those in this category, there would be no role for editors, coaches, critique partners, or one honest friend.

Christian writers often believe, "If God calls me to a task, he will take me through the task." I believe this—about the practice of writing. I've often experienced the Lord's influence as I've struggled with an article or book chapter. But the insight God provided or the Scripture I felt he led me to examine *informs* what I write. The experience is seldom (read that as *never*) a complete page-by-page dictation from heaven.

For some writers, their conviction is so strong they refuse to accept feedback which suggests their storyline requires strengthening, or their writing skills need improvement. They ignore suggestions to attend classes, join a critique group, or retain a writing coach. The disappointment can progress to discouragement—and sometimes turns to anger or resentment. "They don't know what they're missing." Or "They'll be sorry when this becomes a bestseller." The one I hear most often? "It's not fair."

What's not fair is to ignore the potential success God might have called us to fulfill because we rejected the requirement to learn the craft. Anyone can write. *Writing well* is the goal.

What's the missing ingredient to achieve the goal? Humility.

One definition of humility I find to be true is: "Humility is an outward expression of an appropriate inner or self-regard."[1] In other words, the ability to see yourself as you are, not who you aspire to be.

Self-awareness is a tough mountain to master. How can we gain the personal perspective we need so our work rises to the top? Let's review a set of tips and tools to take us to the summit.

- Submit: The first step to moving forward is to *submit* both ourselves and our work to the development process. Once we acknowledge the need to develop our skills, practices, and perhaps most vital, our expectations, the journey becomes far more manageable.

- A critique partner is a good start. Who among your writer friends might be a good fit? Truth-telling is an absolute requirement, candid but kind. Search for a candidate who can offer positive feedback as well as areas for improvement. Best partners are those who share ideas to strengthen the writing versus someone who focuses on what doesn't work.

- Consider working with a qualified writing coach. A coach can help strengthen your work and preserve your "voice." Some coaches focus their practice on specific genres. Others may specialize in proposal writing, preparing the pitch, or guiding clients to the best publishers for their work. Their knowledge builds yours.

- Education: Stay on top of learning opportunities. The industry is changing at lightning speed. Publishing house consolidation has impacted writers. Be aware of changes in the business of writing.

- Engagement: Writing is often a solitary sport, and isolation can prompt self-reliance.

- Writers who live in an echo chamber may struggle to accept feedback and become reluctant to share their work with others. Individuals who lose objectivity about the quality of their writing are often closed to critique, suggestions, or improvement ideas. Might that be you?

Today's writing world is expanding every day! Podcasts devoted to writers of every genre, online classes, tutorials from experts, conferences, and professional organizations for writers are available.

Many agents and publishers have created websites, blogs, or social media pages that provide answers to questions about the craft and the industry overall. These professionals offer insight into the business side of writing.

Comradery and connection with other writers are valuable. We all face many of the same challenges. As the adage goes, "misery loves company." The chance to commiserate about disappointment or discouragement gives us a safe outlet for our frustration. We all need someone to help talk us off the ledge and point us toward the keyboard once again.

We boost our creativity when we brainstorm, share tips and ideas, and serve as cheerleaders for one another. Creativity also inspires hope. We learn to celebrate, rather than envy, our friends' success and believe if we choose to refuse to throw in the towel, we, too, will find victory.

Humility is the secret ingredient to growth and development in this life, no matter what your goal may be. So the next time someone offers you a slice of humble pie, ask for a big piece!

NEXT STEPS:

Read through the four bulleted opportunities above and identify which may be your key to greater success and growth.

AND—IT'S A NO FROM ME

SHARON TEDFORD

> Let us hold tightly without wavering to the hope we affirm, for God can be trusted to keep his promise. Let us think of ways to motivate one another to acts of love and good works. And let us not neglect our meeting together, as some people do, but encourage one another, especially now that the day of his return is drawing near.
>
> —Hebrews 10:23-25 NLT

Twenty-seven publishers rejected the unforgettable work of Dr. Seuss. The ever-popular *Chicken Soup for the Soul* met with one hundred forty-four "not today, thank you" letters.[1] The silvery voice of Tori Kelly didn't make the final rounds of *American Idol*.[2] Elvis Presley was snubbed by a band manager, who told him he'd better go back to driving trucks.[3] When Vincent Van Gogh died in 1890, he'd sold *one* painting![4]

We all know the sting and burn of rejection. If you've ever submitted any work for critique, you understand the feeling of being turned away. Rejection is not easy. In fact, pretty repulsive is an accurate description.

I don't know about you, but my stomach churns every time I read (yet another) rejection letter.

I've wanted to give the "offending" editor or event organizer a call to remind them what a *fantastic* opportunity they have missed. I've even written an email or two with snarky tones, expressing my disquiet at what I perceived as their mistaken rejection. However, you'll be pleased to know I deleted the emails before I hit Send.

Perhaps you've responded in the other way I've reacted? (Yes, I'm a multilingual whiner!) I've berated myself with a reminder I'm not good enough anyway. I've told myself to get back in my box and give up on this mission—so stupid, indeed.

As Christians, we are not immune to rejection or from the pain this brings. We can be hurt as easily as the next person.

However, we can make significant changes to our responses.

How do we handle the potential rejection wound? How can we maintain the sense of God's call on our lives and not be put off by the world's no thank you?

The Scripture above gives us a good clue of how we ought to respond when we feel snubbed.

Most important is to remember our hope is in God and in him alone. Our hope should not be in our work. God sees our hearts. Yes, he has called us to different acts of service and ministry through various mediums. But his greatest desire is we love him, not that we get a contract to speak, cut a record, or publish a book.

If we've pitched our work to a Christian publication, we may be communicating with an editor or publishing house representative who's a brother or sister in Christ. This passage in Hebrews is clear as Scripture outlines how we should talk to them. We are to "motivate one another to acts of love and good works" (v. 24) and "encourage one another" (v. 25).

The writer to the Hebrews wouldn't much like my snarky emails filled with mutters and moans. He would much prefer I bless those who choose not to take on my work.

How should I do that? The answer is simple and available in abundance.

I pray.

Yes, I pray for those professionals who choose to go another way. They have picked someone else's work over mine. I trust God, in his sovereignty, will be glorified whatever their decision. I pray for the increase of his kingdom no matter whose work they accept.

And if they've sent suggestions for improving my work, I pray I will have discerning humility to know how to receive their constructive criticism.

In addition, I can thank them in an email or letter. I can encourage the anonymous publishing house Christian sibling on the other end of the computer by blessing them and not cursing them. I imagine they don't get too many happy emails in response to rejections. Let's start a new trend—let's be the "contented rejected" and respond with kind words to build others up.

NEXT STEPS:

Let's pray.

Lord Jesus, I know you've called me to this work. You've invited me to _____ (write, speak, sing) and I'm certain you have an assignment with my name attached. Although this wasn't to be my appointment, I'm grateful there is a task set aside for me. I wait with patient expectation for that project to be revealed. Let's search this out together, Lord.

I ask you to bless _____ (sender's name on refusal letter), and I pray you will fill his/her day with your joy. He/she is my fellow worker in the kingdom, and I am thankful for the opportunities you're giving him/her to spread the good news of Jesus. In the power of the Holy Spirit, I stand beside him/her today as a fellow soldier for Christ. Lord, may he/she know your smile of delight today. Amen.

THE POWER OF HEALING

KAREN DEARMOND GARDNER

Those who are wise will take all this to heart; they will
see in our history the faithful love of the LORD.

—Psalm 107:43 NLT

Has God ever asked you to do something you didn't want
to do? I'm pretty sure we can all raise our hand on that one.
The impression from God seemed clear.

Write a book.

I knew what he meant—he wanted me to tell the world
my story. A story I resisted sharing. Besides, I knew nothing
about writing a book.

At my first writers' conference, I pitched the book to a
publisher. As I approached him, my knees were shaking
as I expected rejection. You could have knocked me over
with a feather when he handed me his business card. He
expressed interest in the ideas behind my book and said,
"so many who write on difficult topics struggle. They pitch
the book but write from a place of anger."

I wasn't angry. But the conference uncovered a chink in
my facade—shame. And the pain I refused to acknowledge
revealed I wasn't ready to write the book.

God attached a promise to his request—*women are
waiting*. But knowing I needed to write the book and the

actual process were two different things. I questioned whether I was the one to write on this topic, but God was clear.

Write the book.

If I had asked him a few questions like "When and how do I write the book?" I could have saved myself from feeling like a failure.

Six months after the conference, God led me to a group to work through the pain I ignored for years. Healing changes how we write about what happened to us. We write from the perspective of what God did with what happened to us, from the view of God's faithful love.

Writing our painful history shouldn't be easy—*it should be hard*. What happened to us becomes chapters in our life. But these chapters are not the complete story, nor are they the ending. The question we must ask ourselves is, "Why are we writing? Is the goal to expose those who hurt us? Are we compelled to write the ugly? Or do we write from a place of healing and freedom?"

Or do we long to tell the story of God's faithful love in our greatest pain?

When we write from a place of healing and share enough of our story, the reader can see themselves in our story's pain and healing.

As we describe the circumstances, our experience becomes more about what God did with our history—not just what our history did to us. The story shifts to God's loyal love, beauty, kindness, and goodness in the middle of our ugly. As we write from this place, the focus becomes less about us and more about helping the ones who don't know healing is possible. Those who may believe what happened to them is a life sentence.

With *wisdom*, you *understand* how to use your story to help the reader on her journey. You also *consider* and discern the best path to respond to her questions. Your story becomes less about you and more about the reader.

As you write the hard, think of all the authors who have gone before you and those who will come after you. Women are waiting to hear how God led you to face the pain, to release the trauma, and how he set you free. Your story comes from a place of hope and not despair.

"Has the Lord redeemed you? Then speak out! Tell others he has redeemed you from your enemies" (Psalm 107:2 NLT).

God wants us to tell our stories of creating beauty out of the ugly! His healing calls us to share with those still stuck in pain. To touch those who can't imagine the splendor. Perhaps God *chose you* to be the one to tell his story of redemption.

The goal is to drive our readers to the One who loves with extraordinary love, to the only One who can set them free through healing.

How can you prepare to write your story?

NEXT STEPS:

- Journal. Every gory and horrible detail of what happened to you. Record the pain, the hurt, how you felt, the rage, the frustration, and all the places God showed up. Include the moments he stepped into your pain, the places he touched and healed.

- Ask Jesus what he wants to say about the hard and what he wants you to share as you tell your story.

- Surrender your story as you write by being open and teachable. God doesn't need an editor, but we do.

ARMOR UP!
THE BATTLEFIELD OF TIME

BECKY CARPENTER

A final word: Be strong in the Lord and in his mighty power. Put on all of God's armor so that you will be able to stand firm against all strategies of the devil.

—Ephesians 6:10-11 NLT

When God takes our spiritual walk to new levels, expect new devils!

The moment God increases *through* us, Satan increases attacks *on* us. Our call to write for the kingdom is not immune to such attacks. When we answer a kingdom call, an uninvited guest eavesdrops on the conversation. This invader attempts to come into our homes, pop a squat in our recliner, jack our joy, elevate our emotions, and ultimately hijack our time.

The thief's purpose is to steal and kill and destroy (see John 10:10).

Time is precious and priceless. We cannot buy, barter, or borrow moments. How we invest our days has a direct impact on our personal faith journey. As writers and speakers, the way we steward our time can also have an eternal impact on the faith journey of others. Whoa! A thought both scary ... and beautiful. Time is a target of a real thief—a thief who throws distractions and detours in our path.

I didn't grow up with a love for reading or writing. In all transparency, I was the student who became friends with Mr. Cliff's Notes. After all, Macbeth did *not* speak the language of this East Texan! I'm sure my teachers would crack a grin if they knew I became an educator.

Fast forward to the year God flipped my life script—the one I'd envisioned. The year I was gut-punched into the wilderness. An unknown world filled with scary—and beautiful—experiences. The place where pain and tragedy produced purpose and passion. My priorities and interests changed in an instant, and my love for reading and writing elevated. God reached down and took hold of me (see 2 Samuel 22:17). He tossed me (kickin' and screamin') right into the arena of ministry. Through his undeniable love and presence, I felt the immediate urgency to share Jesus in a way people like me can understand—simple, real, and raw!

Speaking and writing became my personal outlets to advance God's message while helping heal my brokenness, an unexpected outcome. What I didn't realize when I answered this call to ministry is the true cost of this assignment. Spiritual attacks!

The more I delivered God's message, the greater the number of attacks. Detours and distractions were the small hits. Health issues, broken relationships, and tragedies were the big ones. I came to realize if Satan isn't attacking, he's content with where we are! Seems he wasn't too content with me! The enemy will stop at nothing to detour us from our kingdom assignments. So, what do we do?

Friends, we must be *watchful* (2 Corinthians 2:11) and *intentional* (Ephesians 6:18). Evil can't win unless we act as though it doesn't exist, or when we are on the defense. We must get on the offense! We must be intentional to stay plugged into Jesus. We must discern the details in the detours and resist the distractions. Learn to discern between a distraction and a divine interruption. When God has called us to speak or write for his kingdom, the assignment is sacred. We must protect and carry out the mission. Resist efforts that take our focus off the Lord's charge. "Set your minds on things that are above, not on things that are on earth" (Colossians 3:2 ESV).

Protecting our time is a battle. A battle we must fight from an offensive position. We battle like warriors in combat—fighting for every hour required to fulfill the kingdom assignments. We must use our God-given weapons. Wearing God's armor allows us to stand firm against the strategies of the devil (see Ephesians 6:11).

Strap on the belt of *truth*, armor up with God's *righteousness*, pull up the bootstraps of *peace,* and hold firm the shield of faith. The enemy doesn't fight fair. He fights with flaming arrows! (see Ephesians 6:14-16). Protect the mind with the helmet of *salvation* and take the sword of the Spirit (*Word* of God) in boldness to the masses! (see Ephesians 6:17).

When we answer our assignment call, remember *who* is on the line. Jesus deserves our undivided attention. He is the giver and guardian of time, the defender of focus, and the officer of truth. He is the great I Am. If I Am is calling, invite him into your calendar and get to writing!

> For I hold you by your right hand, I, the LORD your God. And I say to you, "Don't be afraid. I am here to help you."
>
> —Isaiah 41:13 NLT

NEXT STEPS:

Time to get on the offense. Read and meditate on John 10:10 and 2 Corinthians 2:9-11. Has your kingdom assignment been delayed due to continuous lies from the enemy? Has the assignment suffered from mental, emotional, relational, or physical challenges? Have you taken those concerns straight to the Father? Spend intentional, continuous time in prayer. Ask God to remove the heavy chains of insecurities. Ask our loving Father to bring focus and protection to your speaking or writing assignment.

THE JOY OF WRITING

Laura McPherson

> Dear brothers and sisters, when troubles of any kind
> come your way, consider it an opportunity for great joy.
>
> —James 1:2 NLT

We are writers because we love to write. Thoughts and ideas flow in and out of our minds. We picture different scenarios, and we enjoy putting pen to paper, fingers to the keyboard, or investigating what words to use. We become close to our characters or concepts. All this brings joy to our hearts and confirms our calling.

Sometimes writers experience situations they don't think they can muster through. We analyze our next steps, and our mind decides the complexity or confusion is too great and doesn't want to continue. We doubt our abilities and think perhaps our skills aren't as good as we thought they were. Our heart says keep going, and our head says maybe not. But then, a soft, steady voice says, stay the course and persevere. I attribute this voice to the Holy Spirit, who tells us to see the circumstances through different lenses. We need to claim our trials and testing as pure joy because they will produce perseverance. Joy supports our creativity.

My mom passed down the joy of writing to me. After my three siblings and I were on our own, she was eager to return to writing. She was a journalism major in college and wrote military history later in her life. She also published several magazine articles. At eighty-five, she published her first book.

Stay the course was a common phrase used centuries ago. Soldiers were encouraged to stay committed to their orders and not defect. Those were the days when soldiers marched in a line in full exposure to the enemy. As writers, can we stay the course and consider our struggles as pure joy?

To stay the course is not about succeeding but about continuing when the process is difficult or complex. My father used to say, "Stay in the direction you've committed to." Today, we can choose to stay the course in many facets of life when we encounter a challenging assignment, hike a steep trail, run a marathon, or when writing a book, article, or screenplay.

As an author, I use this phrase to keep going and push through discouragement, self-doubt, deadlines, naysayers, procrastination, and other obstacles. The enemy is famous for inflicting self-doubt and discouragement on those who know God called them to write. Declaring James 1:2-3 is our answer. Joy is the answer to many of our difficulties. Welcoming trials can be hard, and you may see joy as a pie-in-the-sky suggestion. Speaking of pie ... let's see how the acronym **PIES** will help us stay the course and return us to the joy of writing.

Prayer aids us in determining our purpose and priorities. We can become confused as we get off track with too many rabbit trails. When you begin a project, pray over your choice and methods.

Inspiration: Where do you get your inspiration? Who or what inspires and encourages you? Scripture is one obvious choice, but what other options exist? Pray for God's Spirit to guide you in all you do.

Expectations: Have you learned to manage your expectations? Are your goals and expectations realistic?

Remind yourself you are called to write. You cannot rush or delay the process.

Statement: Find a message, phrase, quote, or Scripture that calms you when anxiety or confusion slips in. Find encouraging quotes, Scriptures, and life-giving statements to help you continue the journey. We can push through obstacles with God's help.

NEXT STEPS:

Read through the text below. Record any thoughts of how you might apply them to your life.

When we embrace and practice humility, the struggle is more manageable. Why? We trust the larger picture for our life. Without a humble heart, we are self-focused. As writers, we may believe we are humble when in fact, we lack genuine humility. This happens when our focus is not on the process but on the end result. Getting caught up in how others perceive us and who we might become is all too easy. We keep our joy intact as we seek to glorify God—and not ourselves—in our work.

Need more joy? Sit down and write!

TIGHTY WRITEY

Michele McCarthy

The words of the Lord are pure words, like silver
refined in a furnace on the ground, purified seven
times.

—Psalm 12:6 ESV

I doubt that to assume writers are avid readers is a
stretch. We relish a catchy turn of phrase. Our minds ponder
proficient, masterful dialog. With eyes closed, we treasure
the magical word picture soaring us beyond our present
circumstances to new possibilities. We believe every written
word we savor came to us with no edits necessary. A big NO.

My writing venture began when a ministry worker
suggested I write my story to encourage others. Deep within,
I knew her words were a God nudge. Thus my journey was
birthed. But while writing my personal story, a children's
book title and idea came to mind. In my mind, this seemed
a less daunting project. Short and simple. Rhythm and
Rhyme. Should be a snap. A simple exercise in learning
the ropes of the publishing process. How much editing can
a short book require?

One definition of the word *edit* is to prepare written
material for publication by correcting, condensing, and
writing tight[1]—or as I say, tighty writey. Yet as writers, we
must recognize edits are more than grammar corrections

or word count reductions. Revisions zero in on *the* perfect word to evoke emotion, paint a picture, or encourage change. Fine-tuning incorporates pizzazz and punch with fewer words. Impactful lines stand on their own. Tighty writey is more than a cute catchphrase—writing tight is a valuable lesson for authors.

Tighty writey feels akin to the manuscript version of Gideon's story in Scripture (Judges chapters 6-7). The Angel of the Lord found Gideon beating out wheat in the wine press, hiding and feeling abandoned by God. As he worked, the Angel of the Lord named him "valiant warrior." God handpicked Gideon to deliver Israel from their surrounding enemies.

You were doubtless minding your own business, laying low, when God beckoned you to write. Your response may have been similar to Gideon's reaction. But ... "My family is the least of the tribes, and I am the youngest." The potential writer version ... "I don't work on the computer. I can't put my ideas on paper."

Not to be deterred, the Lord told Gideon he would be with him. And he is with you as well. When God calls, he qualifies.

Gideon begins with an army of thirty-two thousand men. The Lord said, "too many," so twenty-two thousand went home. Again, the Lord said, "too many," so the Lord tested the way the men drank water from the creek and sent all but three hundred home. Gideon had to whip his head back and forth while he watched man after man depart his army. Did Gideon doubt God's methods? God whittled down Gideon's troops like a log shaved into a pencil. In turn, God received greater glory.

Editing and reediting ad nauseam feels like stripping our creation down to its skivvies. Shaving our manuscript from a tome to an essay. Gideon was left to fight the Amalekites and Midianites—with a platoon of three hundred instead of the military force of thirty-two thousand men.

Praise God we aren't fighting a physical war. But we are battling for our articulation to glorify God. We contend for the right title, best cover, correct publisher, and the perfect platform. The special attention we give to our writing process is vital. Writing important messages using as few words as possible is key. Rewriting and editing are our version of whittling—wincing as hard-earned phrases and sweat-derived paragraphs hit the cutting room floor. Sounds like clipping thirty-two thousand words to three hundred.

We must learn to appreciate the editing process. Let's welcome the process to clarify our message with less discourse. Solomon gives us a great reminder with his challenge in Ecclesiastes to let our words be few (see Ecclesiastes 5:2). We can refine and streamline our message. God's glory increases because of our obedience.

NEXT STEPS:

Check out Word Hippo (https://www.wordhippo.com) for synonym ideas. Replace several of your go-to phrases with a single word.

FOLLOW WHO?

DONNA NABORS

Jesus said to him, "If it is my will that he remain until
I come, what is that to you? You follow me!"

—John 21:22 ESV

I want to be her—she has great insight in sharing God's
Word so everyone can understand.

I want to be her—she spins a fiction story with such ease.

I want to be her—she writes inspiring devotions.

I want to be her—she always knows what to say and
how to pray.

I want to be her—everything she writes touches the heart.

I remember playing follow the leader as a child. One child
was the leader, and the next person in line had to follow
what the leader did, and the pattern continued on down the
line. The first child behind the leader got the pattern right,
but somewhere along the line, something changed.

As adults, we still play follow the leader. We have
mentors, those we admire and aspire to replicate. If we want
to be like them, we follow what they do. But sometimes, we
follow the wrong leaders, resulting in the wrong actions.
So, who should we follow, or should we follow at all?

Throughout the New Testament, Jesus said, "Follow
me." Each time, he had a specific purpose in mind.

Jesus used two Greek words in the gospels when he said, "Follow me" (sometimes translated "come"). Jesus used the first one with a sense of urgency—*Follow* or *come now*.[1] The other depicts an invitation to follow as a disciple, much like we might follow a leader and imitate their actions.[2]

Scripture shows a sense of urgency in three ways.

First: A New Purpose

> And he said to them, "Follow me, and I will make you fishers of men." —Matthew 4:19 ESV

Jesus set forth a new purpose for these men. They would no longer fish to satisfy the physical, but they would follow him and fish to satisfy the soul. He has a purpose for each of us as well.

Second: Rest

> And he said to them, "Come away by yourselves to a desolate place and rest a while." For many were coming and going, and they had no leisure even to eat. —Mark 6:31 ESV

Jesus understood the need for rest and knew when the requirement was immediate. We need rest. We are not superwomen.

Third: Refresh and Restore

> Jesus said to them, "Come and have breakfast." Now none of the disciples dared ask him, "Who are you?" They knew it was the Lord.—John 21:12 ESV

After this meal, Jesus reaffirmed his purpose for Peter three times, just as Peter had denied him three times. Peter was refreshed with a meal, and Jesus restored him to ministry. When we stop and refresh by spending time with Jesus, we walk away reaffirmed and ready to move forward.

We can follow a leader in three ways.

First: Leave Others

As Jesus passed on from there, he saw a man called Matthew sitting at the tax booth, and he said to him, "Follow me." And he rose and followed him.—Matthew 9:9 ESV

In the gospels, Jesus called the disciples to leave behind their former lives and follow him. God may not ask us to leave our homes and family, but he does ask us to leave behind what hinders our walk with him.

Second: Leave Self

Then Jesus told his disciples, "If anyone would come after me, let him deny himself and take up his cross and follow me.—Matthew 16:24 ESV

Jesus loves us. Because of his love, he also asks us to leave self behind. We replace our desires with his desires as we follow him.

Third: Follow His Voice Where He Leads

My sheep hear my voice, and I know them, and they follow me.—John 10:27 ESV

When we spend time in prayer and Scripture, we come to know his voice. Where he leads us might not be where he leads someone else.

Jesus still says, "Follow me." He still has a specific purpose in mind for each of us. He doesn't call us to write like someone else but to write what he calls us to write.

Who do you want to be? Who are you following?

I want to be who Christ wants me to be. I want to follow Christ alone.

NEXT STEPS:

The call is to follow Jesus and discover his purpose for you as a writer. Find a like-minded accountability partner. Ask for their commitment to keeping you on track with your purpose.

TRIPLE TRUTH

SHARON TEDFORD

Jesus told him, "I am the way, the truth, and the life.
No one can come to the Father except through me."
—John 14:6 NLT

We've all attended the party where the most animated person on the dance floor was the one with no rhythm. They flail their arms around in frantic windmill fashion without a care in the world. They're committed to their dance but less committed to the tempo of the song. Everyone looks on in amusement.

Funny to watch, perhaps, but the truth is, we are often disturbed by a person whose dance is devoid of rhythm. One who is always ahead of the tempo or lags behind is a distraction.

Why? Because I believe God created us to enjoy rhythm and love cadence. Repeated patterns surround our lives, and there is great comfort in the pulse, shape, and map of life.

We enjoy poetry and rhyme because they meet our hearts' innate expectations for familiar comfort, and our brains find the organized structure attractive.

When we see someone who dances with a disregard to the beat or read a poem showing contempt for the work's rhythm, we feel uncomfortable. God designed us for order and harmony, and most of us enjoy sequences. I put this quick rhyme together:

> There was a young lady from Spain,
> Who never could dance in the rain,
> It made her hair crazy,
> All bouncy and wavy,
> So, she stayed inside and never went out if there was a cloud in the sky.

How did that feel? Good? Or do you want to take me by the throat and share a brief disgruntled word in my ear? The final line is a disappointment because we expect the limerick to flow and catch the wave of the rhythm set up in the first part of the piece. But instead of a joyful ride on a surfboard, I slammed you against the coastal rocks of frustration with the last line packed full of dissatisfaction.

Poetry writers must pay attention to rhythm and rhyme. We can either bless our readers with a beautiful journey of lilting nuances or disenchant them with a broken-down bus of painful disillusionment. We influence the experience they have—let's make the encounter a great one.

Pay attention to the number of beats or syllables in each line of the poem. If you create a pattern, stick to the form. Be thoughtful about the way you use a rhyming scheme. And again, keep to the structure you create.

If you are one of those people who want to tip their toe on the lawn when the sign says, Keep off the Grass, and you're desperate to be a rhythm or rhyme rule-breaker, go ahead. Just make sure your broken rules don't lead to broken hearts. Be certain there's a clear and obvious reason for the apparent malfunction. A literary surprise can be fun.

To prose writers or speakers, cadence applies to you too, so don't nod off.

The Scripture at the beginning of this piece has a twofold purpose. The first job is to alert us to the joy of threes. When we speak or write in threes, the mysteries of the pleasures of regularity come to life.

Look at the three used in this verse: "I am the way, the truth, and the life." I wonder if you learned this familiar passage as a young child. The elegant pulse of this Scripture is easy to grasp. Jesus makes a list of three—and with a hop, skip, and a jump, he draws us on to a finite and important conclusion—the only way to the Father is through the Son.

We can say the same when we write, speak, or present and use rhythmic timbre; we'll highlight our end goal, and the *point* of our writing will shine like a polished diamond.

The second reason I used this Scripture here is to remind us of the joy rhythm brings to our spiritual lives.

Sometimes we might search, study, and explore a biblical topic for a written piece and then want to consider our investigation as our personal Jesus time. I have been guilty of this, and the result wasn't pretty. Our kind God wants us to gather good food for ourselves before we give any away to others. Just as the cabin crew says every time they board a flight: "in the event of an emergency, please put on your own oxygen masks before you assist others."

When I get in a good rhythm of intentional Bible study with the holy three, my life will have order, rhythm, and pattern. The rhyme of my life will be attractive to others, and they'll want to listen to the whole poem of God's story.

Will you join me in the search for rhythm and rhyme in both your creative work and your spiritual life? Let's be those who use our lives *and* compositions to attract others to Jesus.

NEXT STEPS:

Practice rhythm and rhyme, and finish the limerick with a flourish:

> There was a young lady from Spain,
> Who never could dance in the rain,
> It made her hair crazy,
> All bouncy and wavy,
> (Insert your rhyming line here!)

HOW MUCH LESS

LORI ALTEBAUMER

> But will God really live on earth among people? Why, even the highest heavens cannot contain you. How much less this Temple I have built!
> —2 Chronicles 6:18 NLT

I love hearing agents admonish authors not to say "God gave me this book" when pitching an idea. I know I shouldn't take pleasure in this moment because I know writers are serious when they say this. But the audacity of such a statement boggles my mind.

The truth in the verse above brings me to my knees in humility every time I read the words. This Scripture passage shares the account of Solomon as he dedicates the temple—the house of the Lord, which he has built. We're told of the structure's grandeur and magnificent appearance. Solomon details the amount of gold, silver, and bronze used as well as the precious stones adorning this mighty structure. He praises the craftsmanship of the artists who created the sculptures, carvings, and tapestries. Every detail down to the bowls and spoons is noted as having been made with excellence and opulence.

And yet Solomon still knew the truth. If the heaven and highest heaven can't contain our God, then no manmade structure on Earth—no matter how beautiful, brilliant, or dazzling—stands a chance. Solomon knew his place.

Now I'm well aware I'm not writing to create a dwelling place for God, but Solomon's sentiment here still resonates. I should strive for excellence as far as my ability allows. I never set out to create a shoddy piece of penmanship, whether in a book, blog, or social media post. Yet even in my best moments, when I feel I've captured and communicated the exact thing God would have me say, I am aware my words are nothing more than a straw hut compared to a temple worthy of being the Lord's dwelling place. The awareness is painful.

This verse reminds me in a powerful way to esteem the value of my creations in the correct way.

By comparison, God told David and then Solomon to build this house. He gave detailed instructions and moved mountains to make this happen. I know he can and does give people books to write.

The problem arises when we forget what Solomon understood.

Solomon knew the incredible structure he'd built was an inadequate offering for his God—a God so big the heavens couldn't hold him.

Solomon continues his prayer with, "O my God, may your eyes be open and your ears attentive to all the prayers made to you in this place" (2 Chronicles 6:40 NLT).

Again, Solomon's plea draws my heart, and I wonder if my efforts to ask God to open his eyes and ears to the prayers I lift for my writing are enough.

- When I pray for direction in what he would have me say on the pages I create.
- When I pray for his anointing on the messages I pen, that they might be for his glory and to bless others.
- When I pray he blows away the wrong or worthless words I expressed like chaff.

- When I pray the words I write be a worthy place for the touch of his glory.

All this and this alone is within my power. Maybe the statement will be true—the Lord gave me the book. But maybe the book was just for me. Perhaps I've built a place for my heart to dwell for a season so the Lord might meet me there. After all, Solomon expressed many times in his prayer of dedication for the people to turn their faces to the Lord's house. Perhaps I can carry the comparison of my writing and the temple Solomon built even further. When I believe in my heart, God gave me the words for a book—the first thing I should do is look for him to speak to me there.

How awesome to know as Christian authors that the work we do, thinking we are ministering to others, is also a sacred time and place where God may minister to us first.

But first, we must accept the true worth of "this house which I have built."

We must embrace our place in God's grand scheme.

NEXT STEPS:

What does 2 Chronicles 6:18 speak to you?

Read 2 Chronicles 6:1–7:6. What emotions do you think Solomon was experiencing here? Compare how you feel about finishing a writing project with how Solomon must have felt about the completion of the temple. How was he able to say, as in verse 18, "Why, even the highest heavens cannot contain you. How much less this Temple I have built!" (NLT) Take time today to write a prayer of dedication for your writing.

BE YOURSELF. EVERYONE ELSE IS ALREADY TAKEN

DEB DEARMOND

I knew you before I formed you in your mother's womb. Before you were born, I set you apart and appointed you as my prophet to the nations.

—Jeremiah 1:5 NLT

Conversation with others often includes a goal or outcome we desire. Talking our way out of a traffic ticket. Building a relationship with someone we admire. Creating an opportunity to help others in a tight spot. Knowing who they are helps direct our voice. If you speak to the traffic cop like he's your little brother, I doubt you would achieve the desired result.

The same is true with authors. "Write what you know" is good advice—and increases in value when you add "and make sure you know who you're talking to." Our writing style, knowledge, and experience help us reach readers. Knowing who they are informs your "voice," and your target audience "recognizes" you.

There are advantages to this recognition as they read our work. They become comfortable with our approach—we speak their language, and the reader opens both heart and mind to our message. Trust builds—and can be instrumental if your work encourages them to adopt a practice, embrace a new approach, or change their perspective on a topic.

As a writing coach, I speak with my clients twice a month. I know their voice—the inflection and type of words that populate their conversation. So I'm always surprised when I receive work submitted for review, which is devoid of their typical style.

It's jarring. I feel confused. Why would they change their approach in their work? Unless the character they're voicing is fictional, this tactic makes no sense.

Have you ever known someone who adopts a "speaking voice" when addressing a group? On occasion, we might be more formal, based on the audience. Years ago, I attended a workshop featuring a local presenter—one I'd heard several times. She was a wonderful speaker—lively, animated, and often humorous.

On this occasion, we were in the south—the Deep South. When she was introduced, I was astonished to hear her speak with a heavy southern accent. At first, I assumed she was just having fun with her audience, believing she'd slip into her normal midwestern style. She didn't. And the faux accent went in and out like a bad FM station. I was stunned and a bit embarrassed for her. Why would she do this? For the life of me, I don't know.

Each of us has a specific design God imprinted in our DNA. His design for us is to live full lives as he created us to do. Writers included.

On occasion, a client will tell me, "I love author LaDee Dah. When I write, I want to sound just like she does." My response is always the same. "The authentic you is better than any cheap knockoff of somebody else." In other words, be real and genuine—and find your voice.

We live in a noisy world. If you're going to be heard, you can't just speak louder. You've got to set yourself apart by demonstrating you have something unique to say in your own unique way.

Do you know your "voice?" Do you know how you sound?

"The writing was down-to-earth, with humor, too."

"This is not a 'head in the clouds' marriage book. It was filled with real-life and down-to-earth examples."

"Not preachy, but a solid, helpful resource."

"The author wrote this book in an approachable tone. Helpful, practical, useful."

This is my voice. My readers recognize me. Those who enjoy my approach will seek me out again. I won't be everyone's favorite—I don't need to be. Other voices, perhaps yours, will draw them in and minister to them in a way I can't.

How do you do that?

Here are some tips to discover your voice.

NEXT STEPS:

- Describe yourself in three adjectives: Example: *transparent, goofy, and loyal.* How can you incorporate those traits into your writing to help readers know who you are?

- Create a profile for the reader you hope to reach. Who are they? Describe in detail, including personality, hopes, needs, style, perhaps culture or age, or anything you think matters.

- Let your personal style shine. Clarity about who you are makes the conversation easier to communicate the real deal about yourself. What sets you apart for the reader? What can you offer?

- Leave the formal tone at work. When you write, express yourself, and communicate from the heart with a desire to encourage, comfort, inform, or challenge. Ask as you write: what is the impact or outcome God wants from this work.

- Write! Then Read What You Wrote. Be honest with yourself: "Is this something I would read and enjoy? Would I subscribe to this blog or buy this author's book?" Is the language too formal? Preachy?

- Resist the temptation to imitate another author's style or attempt to sound writerly.

You are the only *you* God created. He alone knows the intent of the mission, gifts, and abilities he imprinted in our lives. Ask his Spirit to reveal his purpose and the call. He spoke over you in the womb. And never forget, God designed us to imitate him—and him alone.

ONE MORE VOICE—YOUR VOICE MATTERS

KAREN DEARMOND GARDNER

I also have decided to write an accurate account for you.
—Luke 1:3 NLT

Do you wonder if your voice matters? There are so many writers. Will what you say matter to anyone? Yet you feel you can't keep your words inside—you're compelled to pour all that's within you onto paper. Is the process worth the time, and will anyone want to read what I write?

Not long ago, I was in this place. I wondered why God wanted me to write a book about surviving and healing from domestic abuse. By the time I was ready to begin, there were already many books on the subject—written by authors with credentials I don't have. But God used the book of Luke as an example to open my eyes and confirm he had qualified me.

Think about how Luke wasn't a disciple of Jesus. Luke didn't know him as Matthew and John had. He was a contemporary of Paul. Some theologians believe Luke may have experienced Jesus like Paul did in Acts 9, including the bright light, the audible voice of Christ, and blindness.

Luke wrote his account of Christ's life, gathered from individuals who had experienced the Lord. His gospel records the greatest number of stories about the women Jesus encountered. Luke recorded details of Christ's life that don't appear in the other gospels. He wrote the story of God the Father running to the prodigal son.

His voice mattered.

Your voice matters, too. You can bring insight no one else can because your story is unique to you.

But you may say, "Who am I? I'm not this, nor am I that. I'd rather melt into the crowd. Let someone else be in the limelight."

Scripture is full of stories of God using the least qualified to accomplish his highest calling. One who stands out as the least likely candidate for God's work is Gideon, found in the sixth chapter of Judges.

I love how the Angel of the Lord greeted him, "mighty hero, the Lord is with you!"

Gideon asked a string of questions—the Angel responded to none.

Instead, he replied, "Go with the strength you have, and *you* rescue Israel because *I'm sending you!*"

Gideon's response is classic, "Who, me? Do you know who I am? I'm nobody."

The Angel's response is even more classic, "I will be with you" (Judges 6:12–16 paraphrased by the author).

God says the same to you.

As the Angel did for Gideon, God will do for you. Here's the heart of the story. The Lord will do his part, and he will reveal your part. You are the one who sits in front of the keyboard typing words and sentences until they become pages, then chapters, and at last, a book. God will impart ideas and words. You'll use your tools for reference and editing. You might consider the support a writing coach may offer to help you write the best book you can.

Ask God all the questions—just as Gideon did. Our questions do not offend God. If God doesn't answer right away, wait. He'll bring revelation at the right time. The

As with much of our Christian walk, fulfilling our creative calling requires a willingness to submit to God's plan. Some days submission comes easy, and our work floats without much effort along the river of living water flowing from our hearts. But on the hard days, we partner in the sanctification process. We remember the Holy Spirit gave us the fruit of self-control, and we must embrace the discomfort of delayed gratification and fix our eyes on the long-term gain for God's glory.

Proverbs 29:17 says, "Discipline your children, and they will give you peace of mind and will make your heart glad" (NLT). We can lovingly correct the child inside us and make playtime a well-earned reward for hitting a goal or bigger milestone each day. When we do, we not only feel the satisfaction of completing our work, but our spirit rejoices with the knowledge our heavenly Father is well-pleased with our efforts.

NEXT STEPS:

Dedicate time in your calendar or planner to the creative endeavor to which God has called you but label the project "Freedom Time." When we walk in our God-given purpose, we experience true freedom!

FIRST THINGS FIRST
PREPARE THE SOIL

DONNA NABORS

Prepare your work outside; get everything ready for yourself in the field, and after that build your house.
—Proverbs 24:27 ESV

My husband tells a story about joining the Boy Scouts and his excitement to go camping with his troop. The Boy Scout motto is Be Prepared. However, on this trip, the leadership failed to prepare.

On my husband's first (and last) Scout camping trip, they set up camp at the bottom of a hill. During the night, clouds broke loose with torrential rains that flooded their tents. Everyone scrambled to pack up and move while cold, wet, and tired. The Scout leaders' lack of preparation affected more than themselves. The downpour affected all the little boys in their care.

Our writing also requires preparation. When writer's block hits, we can follow the advice of many who suggest we plant ourselves in the chair and not get up until we write *something*. We can follow the advice of writing a bad piece—just to get started. Both suggestions have value, but I would like to provide another thought. *Perhaps we aren't prepared to write.*

Alexander den Heijer, a Dutch inspirational speaker, said, "When a flower doesn't bloom, you fix the environment in which it grows, not the flower."[1]

This reminded me of the parable of the sower and the seed. This story is all about the soil. What type of soil is in my heart? If my writing is not blooming and producing fruit, the single way to fix the problem is to fix my environment—the soil of my heart.

In Luke 8:4-15, the sower scatters seed.

- Some seeds fall by the wayside. This is shallow ground where they are trampled down, and the birds of the air devour their meal.
- Some seeds fall on rock, have no roots, and wither.
- Some seeds fall among thorns and are choked.
- Some seeds fall on good ground, spring up, and yield a crop a hundredfold.

The difference in the yield or the bloom is *the soil.*

The first soil is *off to the wayside* and *not connected to the fertile ground* for planting. The soil of my heart must connect with other believers. This is where I receive encouragement and support so the devil can't steal what I hear by using discouraging voices in the world.

The next soil *rests on rocks where no roots can develop.* Moisture from the living water of Christ must soften the soil of my heart. Roots can then develop as Christ pours into my life through prayer and abiding in his words.

The third soil is *full of thorns.* When the world's cares, riches, and pleasures entangle my soil, my calling is strangled. My life and my writing don't bloom. I must replace my selfish desires with his desires, which are always better.

The final soil is the *fertile soil* where Scripture comes alive. This is where God gives the increase.

How do I prepare fertile soil?

- Seek like-minded Christian friendships.
- Spend time in prayer and Scripture study.
- Make a commitment to God's calling to write.
- Put Christ first, not me.

As I prepare the soil, writing for him grows naturally. I produce fruit, and he multiplies the yield a hundredfold. Fertile ground becomes holy ground.

In Luke 9:44, Jesus says, "Let these words sink into your ears" (ESV). When we prepare our soil, we bury his words in our hearts by what we hear and then pour them out in our writing. We are told to hide his words in our heart—but we can't hide them in shallow, rocky, thorn-infested ground. We must first prepare the soil.

Luke 6:48 talks about the man who digs deep to lay the foundation of his house on the rock. In this passage and others, we notice that Scripture illustrates both preparation and encouragement.

- Noah prepared the ark at God's direction.
- John the Baptist prepared the way of the Lord.
- Jesus said he went to prepare a place for us (John 14:2).
- Ephesians 2:10 says we were created for good works, which God prepared beforehand.
- Second Timothy 3:17 says we are to be prepared for every good work.
- First Peter 3:15 says we should be prepared to give a defense.

NEXT STEPS:

Are you prepared for what God has called you to do? Review the different soil types and consider where your writing is planted now. Spend a few minutes reflecting on the following.

List names of other believers you are connected to who offer encouragement in your call to write.

Choose a time each day to plant your roots deep through prayer and study of the Scriptures.

Pray and ask God to show you the cares of this world that distract and take time from what he has called you to do.

Commit to cultivating fertile soil in your life and writing.

ARE YOU SURE, GOD?

BECKY CARPENTER

> Jesus looked around and saw them following. "What do you want?" he asked them.
> They replied, "Rabbi" (which means "Teacher"), "where are you staying?"
> "Come and see," he said.
> —John 1:38-39 NLT

If you were a fly on the wall during my Jesus chats, you might hear a whole lot of questions. Questions about life, struggles, the weather, or if I'm supposed to be writing and what I'm supposed to be writing. To be frank, God and I have chatted about *all these things*.

When life gets messy, I speed dial my Jesus! After all, Scripture tells us to "pour out your heart to him, for God is our refuge" (Psalm 62:8 NLT). Pouring out our hearts doesn't mean we can't also ask questions. In fact, Isaiah 55:9 assures us God's ways are higher than ours, and our thoughts are not his thoughts. In simple terms, God is way smarter than us, friends! I'm thinkin' we want to seek counsel, guidance, and answers from the one who is smarter than us. And I'm thinkin' he expects us to have questions—many more. What do you think?

Do you hesitate before asking God questions—especially when it appears you're questioning his will? Maybe in doing so, we think asking questions minimizes our trust in the Father. But that's not what Scripture says.

Jesus asked questions. He asked questions of his disciples, complete strangers, individuals, and various groups. He even asked a question of God.

One of the most profound questions in the Bible takes place at the cross. This cry is not only a fulfillment of Psalm 22:1 but also a powerful display of "pouring out your heart," as mentioned above. Jesus, fully human, poured out his heart to the Father as a question. When our questions are coming from a sincere heart, God welcomes such intimacy. Such closeness is displayed in this passage.

> At about three o'clock, Jesus called out with a loud voice, "*Eli, Eli, lema bachthani?*" which means "My God, my God, why have you abandoned me? Matthew 27:46 (NLT)

Have you questioned God? Have you questioned the call God has placed on your heart, wondering if he's forsaken you as you face yet another rejection letter or disheartening review? Yeah, me too!

Here's the good news. God is okay when we ask questions. In doing so, we are not minimizing our reverence toward our Father. Instead, we are strengthening our intimacy with him.

In John 1:35-39, Jesus initiated the interaction with his disciples by first asking a question. Jesus looked around and saw them following. "What do you want?" he asked them (v. 38 NLT). In another passage, Jesus stopped when he heard two blind men shout, "Lord, Son of David, have mercy on us" (Matthew 20:31 NLT). "When Jesus heard them, he stopped and called, "What do you want me to do for you?" (v. 32)

Jesus wanted them to ask for what they wanted from him! Story after story shows Jesus drawing the questions out of his followers and the wounded hearts he encountered.

God already knows our needs. He knows our thoughts. He already knows we have questions. And he knows our heart's desire to ask these questions. And as the loving Father he is, he wants to answer us.

Many times, God answers our questions through the Scriptures. After all, "For the word of God is alive and powerful ..." (Hebrews 4:12 NLT). When we read and meditate on Scripture, we find revelation from the power within the pages in God's Word. Sometimes he answers us through the working of the Holy Spirit within us. When we go to the Lord in prayer, seeking answers by pouring out our hearts, the Holy Spirit works within to reveal the answers.

With God, we find the answers—including the questions regarding the calling God placed on our hearts.

When we have a deep desire to know the answer to our questions, confusions, and uncertainties, the Father pulls our hearts closer to him. After all, we are God's children. Even as adults, we still do not have all the answers. However, we know who does. Jesus can take the most devastating chapters of our lives and flip the script. He rewrites our stories and creates the most beautiful endings, endings filled with victories—though we may not see them until we get Home.

I suspect when you ask God if you are to write about these victories, the answer will be a decisive Yes!

NEXT STEPS:

- Step away from the crazies and chaos and experience complete stillness. In the stillness, seek answers about your calling.

- Take intentional quiet time with the Father. Start by allocating one hour of uninterrupted time with you, your Bible, and the Lord.

- Make sure this time is away from people, cell phones, and other distractions. Use this hour for prayer and intentional time in Scripture.

- Ask God direct questions about the calling he has placed on your heart. What is the Holy Spirit revealing to you?

A WINNER AFTER ALL

LORI ALTEBAUMER

> Wherever your treasure is, there the desires of your
> heart will also be.
>
> —Matthew 6:21 NLT

And the winner is ...

Not me.

I had the new dress and high hopes. I had a seat on the front row, so when my name was called, I'd be ready. My tribe of friends gathered around me—fellow writers who often showed more faith in my abilities than I did.

As one of five finalists in three prestigious award categories at a distinguished writing conference, surely, I might hear my name called at least once. The honor of selection as a finalist with my first novel was a cause worthy of celebration. Receiving an actual award wouldn't hurt either.

But as the categories came and went without my name being called, I found myself faced with a choice.

> Wherever your treasure is, there the desires of your
> heart will also be.
>
> —Matthew 6:21 NLT

I looked at the people around me, cheering me on with great enthusiasm.

These were people who had changed or given up other

plans to be beside me on such an auspicious evening. They were the ones who had encouraged, challenged, and made me believe the award was possible.

A fancy plaque with my name inscribed would be a shallow substitution for the friends I've made on this writing journey.

The world is the domain of the father of lies and screams out the message winning is all there is. The world measures our worth by the earthly treasures we accumulate. But when hard times come, those prizes we fought so hard to acquire won't be there to catch our tears, hold our hand, or make us feel loved when all we feel is hopelessness. When hard times come, the world moves on to the next best thing without another thought.

And yet the world continues to press upon us the lie that *things*—wealth, success, or fame—must be our measuring stick at all costs.

Even at the expense of our hearts.

As Christian authors, we must reflect on what we sow into our hearts.

Before we ever put pen to paper or fingers to keyboard, we must decide where our treasure is. If we don't have a clear and true vision of this, the enemy will soon come to distort our view and pull us away from our original purpose—of honoring the Lord with our gifts.

Excellence in our work honors the Lord when our motivation is right.

How do we pursue excellence and retain a focus pleasing to the Lord?

We demonstrate this in community with others who pursue the same goal. We do so surrounded by a body of believers who challenge us, teach us, hold us accountable, and encourage us as we strive to become more Christlike with our every breath. We align with others who affirm this truth: when God gets the glory, there's no concern about who gets the recognition.

Even among the best intentions of our peers, we can

receive the message that bestseller lists, awards, and multi-book contracts are the goal. But this is not what we find in Scripture. And with Scripture alone, we can dismantle those lies and replace them with the truth of why we do what we do—and for whom we serve.

When we take God's Word to heart, memorize the words, and let them be our guide through the maze of pitfalls on our writing journey, Scripture will always lead us in the right direction. We must stand firm on the truth as our hearts stir for the only treasure worth seeking.

Yes, I had a decision to make that night, but my choice was an easy one. A certificate or plaque wouldn't have cared one bit if I left the award alone in my room, tossed it in the trash, or pinned a medallion to the front of my dress for all to see.

My friends cared. They cared I wasn't discouraged or disappointed. They cared as I planned for my next steps—I knew there was still work to do. And they planned to hold me accountable for living up to God's best for me.

They cared. I spent the evening surrounded by people who didn't require my winning an award to find me worthy of their love.

These were the people who loved me for me. My hands might have left the auditorium empty that night, but my heart was full. I harbored no doubts about where my true treasure was.

I was a winner, after all.

NEXT STEPS:

Pray and consider what is most important to you about your writing. Is that the treasure you have set your heart upon? How does this line up with the treasure God has for you? What does Scripture say?

MY NEW FAVORITE

DEB DEARMOND

Pay careful attention to your own work, for then you
will get the satisfaction of a job well done, and you
won't need to compare yourself to anyone else.
—Galatians 6:4 NLT

With the release of a new book, authors pay close
attention to the reviews to get a "read" on the response to
their work. I'm one of those authors. In the early weeks after
release, several times a day, I log in and check the reviews.
The process is similar to showing up at church with your
new baby so your friends can give your sweet bundle the
once over. You labored in pain, pushed through the birth,
and now the results are on display for everyone to see—and
comment on. I recall my always-appropriate mother once
stepping back from a red, wrinkled, squawking bundle of
joy and exclaiming, "Wow! Now that's a baby!" Her remark
was the kindest words she could muster in the moment.

That's typical of the information you may receive on
your book baby. Some days, you feel pretty good about the
work. Other days, not so much. And the perfectionist in me
can fixate on the few not-so-great ones. I often checked
my reviews but also those of books similar to my topic. I
wanted to know how I fared against the *competition*. God

pulled me up short on this practice, and I was clear—he was not pleased. I'm *one* purveyor of the Lord's message, not the *sole representative* on the topic. He's called others to join the chorus, too.

When I published my second book, I knew the ropes of reviews and ratings—and the importance they play for an author. The impact on sales can be significant, as publishers consider these measurements when authors submit future work for publication.

Each time I opened a new review, I held my breath. I've been blessed no one has taken to my bouncing baby with a hatchet or an ax to grind. On a five-point rating scale, you pray for reviews in the four or five-star category.

But today, I received a new favorite. A *three-star* favorite.

The review caught me off-guard. Three stars is not a disaster, but I'd never dipped below fours and fives. I didn't recognize the reader's name, and she indicated she'd received the book free through a reader's program. Folks receive books they'd never choose. As a result, faith-based authors, on occasion, find folks are unhappy we reminded them about God.

But this reader titled her review as follows: "Helped Me Realize a Thing or Two." My interest was piqued, and anxious curiosity bubbled in my stomach. Here's what she said:

> I'm not usually into self-help relationship books based on religion, but this one seemed like a good fit for my situation. I picked this up weeks before my husband plopped down divorce papers on the counter, so ... yeah. There's that.

> There was a lot of helpful advice here to take—religious or not. The religion stuff didn't bother me as much as I thought it would. Sometimes life sweeps you up and drops you both on your backside, and all you can think about is the stressful parts of life. You lose sight of the fact this person is here because they decided to dedicate their life to helping you. To being there for you.

Yet it's so easy to push them away. To say we're fine when we're not.

I still choose my husband today, and he still chooses me. Beyond that, we'll have to figure it out. But I am thankful I decided to pick up this book.

And so, she helped me realize a thing or two...

God is at work in my work. When I'm sitting at the computer, I have the Christ-following reader in my head. I thought I was writing only to the believer. God has a bigger plan in mind, and my hands on the keyboard belong to him for his purposes. He sees every reader as a candidate for kingdom principles. I needed to understand—and remember—this.

Five-star reviews are great, but ministry is the point. Whether the reader's a Christ-follower or not, I write to point others to the Lord and his love for us. Period. Not to entertain or impress, but to draw them closer to an intimate connection with God. I must resist the urge to compare my work or reviews with others.

Since ministry is the point, the Lord holds me accountable to that commission.

There are days when getting the words on the page is demanding and difficult. Getting the *right words* on the page must always be my standard. He won't settle for less. Neither will I.

So thank you, three-star lady. Today—and maybe for many days still to come—you are my new favorite.

NEXT STEPS:

Ask yourself these questions:
- Do I compare my writing to others? If so, why? What do I gain? What damage might the comparison create?
- What steps do I need to take to see writing as my calling and an extension of ministry?

REJECTION AFFECTION

MICHELE McCARTHY

The heart of man plans his way, but the LORD establishes his steps.

—Proverbs 16:9 ESV

The English language is full of catchy oxymorons. Three of my favorites: Deafening silence. A new classic. Definite maybe.

Rejection affection sounds like a fine fit in the "roll your eyes" category. After all, who holds affection for a rejection? Who embraces the thumbs down? Who champions dismissal?

Christians are familiar with Scriptures appearing to contradict human instinct. To live, we must die. The last shall be first. The adult needs to be like a child. But rejection affection—is that concept in Scripture? Perhaps.

Rejection isn't for cowards. Refusal stings. Dismissal from an agent or publisher of our *baby*, our words—those called, counted, and culled—feels devastating. Spurning our message, birthed through hours of writing and rewriting, could elicit one of two responses—a temptation to throw in the towel altogether or disregard a directive God may be alerting us to notice.

Writers are not exclusive members of the "I am in water above my head" club. The Bible is replete with men and women called to step out of their comfort zone to accomplish a God-sized task. Staying the course despite disapproval and death threats could not have been easy. The task wasn't easy then—or now.

God had a message for Jeremiah to give to Israel and Judah. Jeremiah dictated those words to Baruch, who then delivered the Lord's scroll to King Jehoiakim. The king tore the scroll into pieces and threw said scroll into the fire. That is some serious rejection. God then asked Jeremiah to reproduce the scroll, and in addition, "many similar words were added to them" (Jeremiah 36:32 ESV). Years of threats, mocking, and rejection never deterred Jeremiah. His obedience to give God's message when and how the Lord directed is an example to us all.

Paul wrote Colossians, Philemon, Ephesians, and Philippians while in a Roman prison. Do you think he ever wondered if his imprisonment absolved him from God's assignment? Did he ever want to curl up in a pity party of exhaustion? Praise God, by the Holy Spirit's unction and guiding, Paul completed the task God assigned him.

What might you or I unintentionally do with the assignment we feel the Lord has laid on our hearts if we become impatient or give up? We must let God be the author of our story.

When you face rejection, take a deep breath, and ask yourself, "Lord, what are you trying to communicate to me right now?"

- Do I need more information?
- Does my work need further editing?
- Are the publishers I have contacted the right fit for the material?
- Is the timing right for the release of my message?
- Are you recommending I choose or take a different perspective?

Hindsight is always 20/20, but I assure you I am more than grateful and much relieved my first attempt at publication was a big N.O. To say my book needed an overhaul is an understatement—word choices, chapter placement, and more reader engagement. God gave me fresh ideas. He introduced me to a writing coach. He opened my eyes to the writing technique of "showing, not telling." I rearranged my manuscript to begin at the end and rewind to work the story forward.

Revisions are never wasted. God's clock runs on perfect timing. After my overhaul, a search for different publishers, and listening to God's voice, God led me to the right publisher at the right time for the message he put on my heart.

Rejection doesn't mean your manuscript isn't worthy or will never be published. Perhaps the timing is an issue. Your project may still need a final polish (or six), as in my case. We may never feel deep affection for rejection, but if we look at the work as God's hand in the process, we can learn to appreciate his desire to bring out the best of the message he has given us. Releasing your work into the Father's hands and his guidance is the absolute best solution. When that occurs, rejection affection won't just be a catchy oxymoron, and "power is perfected in weakness" will make perfect sense.

> But he said to me," My grace is sufficient for you, for my power is made perfect in weakness." Therefore I will boast all the more gladly of my weaknesses, so that the power of Christ may rest upon me.
>
> —2 Corinthians 12:9 ESV

NEXT STEPS:

Ask several friends to give you an honest evaluation of your work. Be willing to receive positive and negative feedback.

DON'T MESS WITH THE WORDS GOD GAVE ME

KAREN DEARMOND GARDNER

Search me, O God, and know my heart; test me and know my anxious thoughts. Point out anything in me that offends you and lead me along the path of everlasting life.
Psalm 139:23-24 NLT

Offense flowed through my veins like a hot poker straight to my heart as I read through multiple notes of changes my editor made to my book. How dare she change and cut my words? This is my subject. What does she know?

I assume she knows more than I do.

Although not easy, I needed to release offense to remind me the editor and I had the same goal—to produce a book readers want to read and can find themselves in. This is not about me. This is about the story—the point every author, whether traditional or self-published, must come to.

As I read the edits, I discovered sweet notes telling me how good, powerful, and life-changing a certain section was. What? Turns out she wanted to bring the best out of me, to shift the focus from me to the reader. Turns out we were on the same page most of the time.

To see sections of your book deleted as repetitive or unnecessary is difficult. The editor's decisions are based on whether there's a fit with the storyline. The changes are not a criticism of what you wrote, but you may feel judged. She changed or deleted sections I felt were important to the story. Turns out she didn't understand what I was saying. I was responsible for rewriting and bringing clarity to my message.

If the editor doesn't understand what you wrote, neither will the reader. This was one of my biggest *aha* moments in the entire editing process. Isn't that the goal? She made me dig deeper, seek wisdom, see beyond myself into the heart of my reader. The thought, *but God gave me the words,* shouted at me. I could also see this part of my story wasn't necessary for my reader to know. I approved the edits and saved the story for another project.

Can you imagine how many words didn't make their way into Scripture? God gives us enough of the story so we can find ourselves *in the story*. Regardless of where we are in life, we can find words that seem to lift off the page as we read them, speaking to where we are. We want a book our readers will devour, markup, and maybe read again.

God may give us the words and ideas. But he is perfect; we are not. His words come through our filter. Our words need to be edited, and that's okay. Even the famous authors who sell millions of books need editors.

My book went through many editing rounds. Before the final version went to the printer, I had one last opportunity to go through the manuscript for a final edit. I found a few issues with formatting and a couple of errors all the editors missed. I, too, hadn't caught them!

As the writer, if you don't understand the sentence, then you can presume readers won't either. I read the passage to a friend, and we worked through the sentence until the section made sense. Without one last look, the sticky sentence would have been in the final version.

Editors are your friend even when they appear to be slashing through your manuscript. That's not to say they get everything right. At times you'll find a decision difficult to leave to the experts. To be clear, I'm not an expert writer, but I am a better writer because of those who took the time to tell me the hard and the good.

"Put me on trial, LORD, and cross-examine me. Test the motives of my heart" (Psalm 26:2 NLT). Trust me on this. God will test your motives throughout your writing journey. We must learn to live unoffended and be open to input. God speaks our language, and we must communicate to our readers in theirs. When in doubt, ask the one who knows all things.

By the end of the editing process, I deleted sections that just didn't fit the storyline. I was surprised I could hit delete with ease and not feel like I was cutting out pieces of my heart. Note the smile here.

NEXT STEPS:

- Take a deep breath!
- Are you ready to practice? Write something residing in your heart. Let the work sit for a day.
- Come back to the piece, reread, and allow the Holy Spirit to show you a better way to write that sticky sentence.
- Ask what you need to delete, add, or change. Invite someone to read and review the work. A critique can be scary, but you will be a better writer in the end.

FINGERPRINTS ON THE PAGE

DONNA NABORS

> When Moses came down from Mount Sinai, with the two
> tablets of the testimony in his hand as he came down
> from the mountain, Moses did not know that the skin of
> his face shone because he had been talking with God.
> —Exodus 34:29 ESV

Fingerprints. We all have them. We leave them everywhere, and we notice those others leave.

Several years ago, we moved into a home with black granite kitchen countertops. I never knew my children touched the countertops so often. Every time they rounded the corner, their prints showed up as they leaned on the counter or grabbed the edge. We also had a glass coffee table when they were young. *What was I thinking?* I should have bought stock in Windex as I worked to remove those fingerprints each day.

We live our lives in a similar way. We work hard to remove the fingerprints.

I was at a friend's house not long ago, and we were discussing how grandkids leave their prints on windows and glass tables. But when we leave them in place, those prints can become a sweet reminder of the time we spent with chubby, little fingers.

Fingerprints leave our unique mark everywhere we go. They identify us. In criminal investigations, fingerprints can place someone at a crime scene, identify a suspect, or solve a mystery.

I've made some poor decisions in my life, and I've also suffered abuse at the hands of others. Each time God has picked me up and brushed me off in his tender way, leaving his fingerprints in place of the mistakes and abuse.

Do I want others to recall my mistakes and failures or the prints of God's grace and mercy? Do I want others to remember me by the scars I've received from other people's prints on my life or by God's prints of love and healing?

When I continually go back and relive my past sorrows, I feel as if I'm using paper towels and glass cleaner to wipe off God's prints on my life.

Most years in May, I make the trek from Texas to the Blue Ridge Mountains in North Carolina for an annual writer's conference. The conference is filled with education, encouragement, and awesome worship. The journey is both a physical and spiritual experience as we spend time with God on the mountain, make new friends and rekindle old friendships, and learn from gifted faculty.

One year in a class I attended, we were assigned writing exercises. Volunteers read what they had written in the moment. I was amazed at the on-the-spot writing. And then the thoughts started—self-doubt and lack of worth. Many wrote with such eloquence and consistency. For a moment, I considered going home to delete all my blogs and start over. I wanted to remove my fingerprints.

The voice of encouragement said, "You have some good ideas." The voice of discouragement said, "You don't write as well as others." There before me—the voice of comparison others had warned me about.

Just as we each have unique fingerprints—unlike anyone else—God's fingerprints on our life are also unique. We're not supposed to write like someone else. He gives us our own stories to tell.

Has God saved you, brought you through a storm, shown you his love? Has he given you his strength, granted you peace, been faithful, or caused you to hope? These are the fingerprints of God on your life. Don't try to wash them away. Let God's fingerprints on your life be your identity. Then share his prints with others.

NEXT STEPS:

Where have you seen his fingerprints in your life? Write what you know. Write what God has imprinted on your heart.

Make a timeline of the events in your life that stand out to you. These might be things others never noticed or knew about but are significant to you. How have you seen God's prints on those events? Pick the one that stands out the most and write a one-page draft outlining God's fingerprints on the experience.

WRITING IS A TEAM SPORT

DEB DEARMOND

Two people are better off than one, for they can help
each other succeed.

—Ecclesiastes 4:9 NLT

"Thanks for cheering me on when I wanted to quit. I'd
have given up without your encouragement."

"Brainstorming ideas with you when my plot line got
twisted helped me get back up and running again."

"The marketing tips you shared using social media
saved me so much time and kept me sane!"

"It takes a village." I'm not sure who coined this phrase,
but I believe this is true for those who write. If you believe
God called you to capture a message for the body of Christ,
walking away is not easy when discouragement hunts
you down. And somewhere in your journey, it will try.
Experience speaking here.

The Lord surprised me when he directed me to write.
I'd been encouraged to do so by friends and family but
dismissed the thought without much consideration. Their
persistence puzzled me. I'd built a successful business,
loved my clients, and the returns were high.

No thanks, I'm good.

But in a time of high emotion, after losing my brother,
God's voice was clear. *Write.*

I couldn't ignore the Lord but had no clue where to start. What I knew about writing could fit in a thimble with room left over to swim. Translation: I knew nothing except I had much to learn. *Could I be successful taking this on in my mid-fifties?*

As a lifelong learner, I knew success was possible. So I searched resources, books, and classes and dove into the deep end.

My first writing project was a website for women ages fifty plus. I knew many gals struggled to find their purpose once the nest emptied. The roles they'd embraced for years had vanished. God used this first writing endeavor to guide and educate me on the craft of writing.

But I didn't work alone.

My sister-in-law, Karen, became my partner, and we created a website titled *My Purpose Now*. The Lord sent us a team of women with knowledge in specific areas of life, perfect for our audience. We covered midlife career changes, health, opportunities to serve God, returning to school, married life for the over-fifty somethings, adult kids, and more.

Our crew became the poster girls for Proverbs 27:17: "As iron sharpens iron, so a friend sharpens a friend" (NLT). We encouraged one another, brainstormed ideas, and shared knowledge to strengthen our skills.

Our squad published twice a week for three years. By then, several team members had books in their hearts they longed to write. I was in that group.

Jumping from a once-a-week post to writing a book was overwhelming. I missed my team and the camaraderie I relied on. I realized the time had come to abandon working in isolation and find some new peeps to help me on the journey.

I attended a writer's conference three hours from home. I'm not sure what I expected, but this one event changed the trajectory of my life.

The conferees were gracious and inviting—more than willing to help close my knowledge gap. No question was too basic or silly for them to answer. They asked about my writing journey and offered help. We exchanged contact information, and they encouraged me to stay in touch. I did.

Two of these experts became friends and mentors. One became my writing coach and stewarded me through my first book. Her knowledge, not only about the craft of writing well, but her experience in the business of writing, helped accelerate my opportunities beyond measure. I believe without the guidance and encouragement she provided, the path to publication would have been a much longer journey.

With the publication of six books, I've never forgotten or forsaken the value of connection with other writers and their impact on my success.

The authors of this book teamed up in this adventure to reinforce this belief.

Living Write Texas (LWT) is our writing tribe. Three Texas women met at an out-of-state writer's conference. Not long after our return, we met for lunch and lamented the lack of a local writing community. We discussed the value of partners, collaborators—women who were invested in one another's work and success. Trusted. Candid. Encouragers.

Michele spoke up. "We could start one. Deb, you have the experience."

My response was quick, "Perhaps, but not on my own." Both promised to take active roles. We each brainstormed potential members to invite with a goal to keep the group small.

Ten women gathered a few months later. None of us knew everyone at our first retreat weekend, but God linked our hearts at record speed. We found support, insight, and information all wrapped in the concept of "iron sharpens iron."

Three years later, members of LWT have authored and published eleven books—including several award winners.

One member is a talented, multi-published songwriter and the creator of an award-winning podcast. All members are actively writing and pursuing publication.

We meet only three times a year but often connect via email and Zoom. Each writer knows there's a tribe ready to offer support whenever needed.

Winning together is a key to success. Don't labor in isolation—create connections. And never forget writing is a team sport.

NEXT STEPS:

- Find a writing group. Check your area for chapters of ACFW (American Christian Fiction Writers), Word Weavers International, or AWSA—Advanced Writers and Speaker's Association. AWSA features a protégé membership level if you are not yet published.
- Consider a virtual meet-up—an online group via Zoom could be a great alternative.
- Consider writers you've connected with at conferences or in writing groups via social media pages.
- If you'd like to read more about creating a tribe of your own, see the resource section at the back of the book. You may discover you, too, can create a writing team!

MAKE LIKE MARY

SHARON TEDFORD

But Mary treasured up all these things, pondering them in her heart.

—Luke 2:19 ESV

People ask me how much time I require to write a song. This question is almost impossible to answer.

Sometimes I hear a rhythmic phrase in a conversation and simply must capture what I hear. I stumble on a word in a newspaper that grows a thought picture in my brain. Maybe a pastor expresses a theological notion with such eloquence, I have to steal the idea. This is when I can't write fast enough, and any flat, portable surface becomes fair note-taking game.

But other days, I sit at my piano with my notebook and Bible open, tiptoeing through my ideas at a snail's pace. I look at my meager offering and ask the Lord to turn my five individual words and two sentences into a song sumptuous enough to feed a whole crowd.

And my guess is, this is your experience too. Days when you gather fast and days when the collection is slower.

Both ways of idea collection are valid and important. And both require pondering if God is to speak through our words.

Ponder.

It's what Mary did.

She could have been so overwhelmed and confused. After all, she was tasked with making sure the Son of God didn't get trampled by a donkey, fall down a well, or swallow a marble. She was intimately involved in the details of Jesus's life from the beginning. And she was there at the end.

Mary could have filled her time with busyness and distraction. Instead, she chose to ponder. She gave space and time to her thoughts and let God into every crack and crevice of her meditations. She took time to mull her circumstances and weigh them up.

The Greek word for ponder can mean to "confer with oneself."[1] I picture Mary cleaning up toddler toys and tending tiny laundry while she talked to herself about the wonder of her child. I imagine her on a grocery trip, with shopping bags from the local delicatessen, as she chews over the latest occurrence in the life of her incredible son, Jesus. Her private conversations with herself invited God in as she chin-wagged with her heavenly dad.

What did God say in response? We don't know. But I believe Mary processed the story of her life and her Savior Son over long periods.

How often do we allow ourselves the space to just sit and ponder? Do we give ourselves the go-ahead to be still and take time to wander through the idea rooms in our brains? Are we brave enough to talk ourselves through our stories, allowing them to blossom into levels of believability not present in their first tender state of immaturity?

So much of what we do as writers happens in the secret sphere of our minds. We ruminate and cogitate over ideas and characters for hours, days, and sometimes even months, unaware. We can miss the validity (and necessity) of this practice.

Let's give our storylines permission to roll around in the dust of our intellectual gardens as they mature and become a reality. We need to hand over head space to our prose, poetry, songs, or speeches. We need to consent to the Holy Spirit's hand as we give him permission to shape our ideas into his.

In the development stages, time is our friend.

And what do we do with all those scraps of inspired intentions? Those mountains of higgledy-piggledy notebooks, envelopes, restaurant napkins, and old receipts covered with precious sentences penned in moments of inspiration.

We organize. (Sorry if this is a bad word in your world! That's okay. Everything's going to be okay.)

Assemble your ideas in one place. Buy and keep a notebook somewhere accessible. Grow the habit of collating your scattered ideas. Then, when you are ready to write, you won't have to waste twenty minutes hunting for the perfect phrase because the ideas are right there in your little book.

And when you write, pay attention to your moments of inspirational brilliance. (Hey, I heard that! Yes! You *do* have moments of brilliance!) If you pen a sentence, paragraph, verse, or stanza you love but later realize the words don't fit, do *not* delete the work—take the chunk of love and plop the words into a document named "ideas that didn't fit, but I couldn't get rid of." Or some such snappy title!

Later, you'll congratulate yourself on this stroke of genius.

God is clear about how we ought to live. His style isn't a *rush-around-get-it-done-right-now* God. He's a *take-a-moment-and-consider-what's-in-front-of-you*, God.

> Be still, and know that I am God.
> —Psalm 46:10 ESV

In the stillness, God wants us to contemplate how powerful he is. He calls us to be ponder-people. Let's be those who "make like Mary" and ponder all things—stories, songs, and talks alike—in our hearts as we allow Christ to rule in everything we do.

NEXT STEPS:

- Buy a notebook to collate all your ideas.
- Schedule a specific time to amalgamate all your ideas into your notebook.
- Create a file on your computer for all your "doesn't quite fit" writing.

AT YOUR WORD, LORD

LORI ALTEBAUMER

> "Master," Simon replied, "we worked hard all last night and didn't catch a thing. But if you say so, I'll let the nets down again."
>
> —Luke 5:5 NLT

The writing journey is not unlike Simon Peter's famous and unsuccessful fishing trip.

Simon was done.

He'd worked all night and had nothing to show for his labor but an aching back, wet feet, and nets in need of mending. He dragged his boat ashore and unloaded his nets.

Most writers who have ever pitched to an agent at a conference have experienced the same feelings Simon must have felt in this moment. Who among us has never considered posting our laptop for sale on eBay? Who has never imagined using that disaster of a manuscript we've spent months or years wrestling with to fuel a bonfire over which we plan to torch every writing craft book we've ever purchased?

Writing is hard.

Writing something others will want to read is even harder.

We thought by this time we would be there already. We read the books, attended the conferences, and seated our backsides in the chair until the cushion became permanently contoured to our expanding derrieres.

But the contracts haven't come. No one has read our work. And we've wiped out a small forest faster than a bark beetle infestation in our attempt.

We've fished all night and caught nothing.

The trouble with being an aspiring author who believes they are called by God to write is turning away from the mission—which can be next to impossible. In unguarded moments, our thoughts travel back to the path etched in our imaginations and paved with prose demanding to be captured on the page. We simply can't not write.

So how do we overcome the doubts about our purpose?

Simon might have assumed he was done that morning on the rocky shore of the Sea of Galilee, dragging his empty nets in dismay. But Jesus had the final say.

As the crowds pressed in to hear him preach, it was clear Jesus was having more success in his work than Simon experienced that morning.

I don't know who Simon thought Jesus was at that moment, but something the Messiah said must have grabbed his attention and gripped his discouraged heart. When Jesus climbed in Simon's boat, asking him to "push it out into the water" (Luke 5:3 NLT), Simon didn't argue.

We don't know why Simon complied, other than when the Lord says row, you row. But like the people of Judea who came to hear Jesus, we can be thankful he did. And we can be even more thankful for what happened next.

Make no mistake—Jesus knew what demanding work went into fishing all night. And he knew exactly how much Simon had to show for his efforts. He understood Simon returned empty-handed and downhearted from laboring all night.

At first, all he asked of Simon was to "push it out into the water" (v. 3), so Jesus could speak to the crowd gathered there. I wonder if Jesus might have thought, *You're a fisherman, Simon. Get back in your boat.*

After all, Simon couldn't catch fish—be they footed or finned—if he wasn't in his boat.

Once Simon had his boat in the water, he was exactly where Jesus could use him. As Jesus ended his teaching, he turned to Simon and said, "Now go out where it is deeper, and let down your nets to catch some fish" (v. 4 NLT).

In his good and perfect timing, he positioned Simon for such a large catch that "their nets were so full of fish they began to tear!" (v. 6 NLT).

As writers, we have all experienced those long dark nights yet find ourselves back on the shore with an aching back and empty net. The experience is disappointing and discouraging, and we may find ourselves ready to sink the boat and sell all our nets.

But have we quit too soon? Is there a possibility Jesus has us floating in the shallows so he can speak through us to a small crowd before he launches us into the deep for a catch so big our nets break?

Simon was willing to try one more time. "If you say so, I'll let the nets down again," was his willing response (v. 5 NLT).

My heart breaks as I watch people give up their passion for writing and abandon their call to share God's truth. I'm certain God's heart breaks as well.

We all, like Simon, must get back in our boats—or the ergonomically correct chair to protect and correct our posture—and persevere until the Lord says, "Now go out where it is deeper" (v. 4 NLT).

NEXT STEPS:

Take a moment to reflect on times you thought about giving up. Did you? If not, what kept you from quitting? What were the results of your perseverance?

Write these thoughts down and keep them in a place where you can refer to them whenever you feel the urge to give up.

JUMPING IN
JESUS JOINS US IN THE DITCH!

BECKY CARPENTER

Do not be afraid, for I have ransomed you. I have called you by name; you are mine. When you go through deep waters, I will be with you. When you go through rivers of difficulty, you will not drown. When you walk through the fire of oppression, you will not be burned up; the flames will not consume you. For I am the LORD, your God, the Holy One of Israel, your Savior.

—Isaiah 43:1-3 NLT

How hot is your fire? Can you relate to Shadrach, Meshach, and Abednego from the book of Daniel? These three bro-friends can teach us a few things. They walked out of a despairing situation with a powerful testimony. Their up-close and personal encounter with the King of Kings has echoed across miles and generations. Their experience, now recorded in God's Word, continues to bring hope and encouragement to many of us.

How about you? Have you experienced an unbearable hot trauma or tragedy? Maybe a life wreck hit your home or family and tossed you into a deep ditch of hopelessness and helplessness? One phone call on the day we lost our precious daughter propelled me into this ditch.

The magnitude of grief elevated my faith walk to seek divine intervention. The undeniable presence of our Savior showed up. Did God's presence manifest in your life because he joined you in the ditch? If so, God has given you a gift to share. He's given you a *testimony*.

For many of us, our reluctance to jump into the writing and speaking arena has everything to do with not knowing where to start and believing we are not qualified. With that, let's set out with a common reason for our hesitation.

Trying to figure out where to begin.

We can launch with the ditch! You know the ditch—the place in life's journey where God *gifted* us our own personal testimony.

I knew the moment I arrived at the horrific scene playing out across the black asphalt that my youngest daughter had run into heaven.

God doesn't always calm our storms, but he calms *us*. God may not remove our circumstances, but he walks us through them. Our testimonies are messages from real people. *Real folks* struggling with real-life wrecks. *Real folks* who found help in our real Jesus! In the authentic ugliness of our sufferings, the relatability of our testimonies will launch the beginning of our call to speak and write for his kingdom.

The next area we should conquer is our insecurity about speaking or writing. Lack of confidence may tempt us to resist moving forward. Doubt about our abilities makes us question our qualifications and credentials. We fall into a secular standard of elevating degrees, certifications, and lengthy résumés as a measure of our ability. However, as followers of Jesus, our measure is simple. Walking in obedience to God's Word and answering the call is the most important requirement.

Throughout Scripture, God uses an assortment of *ordinary* people to share his messages. Not only ordinary, but he also uses broken individuals. Even the original disciples would be viewed as less than qualified by our current world standards.

One of my favorite examples of God using the broken is the story of the Samaritan woman at the well in John 4. Most would describe this account as a rich example of redemption and acceptance. However, her story also models courage. This ordinary and shattered woman had the courage to return to her town, where she was likely viewed as a social outcast, to reveal her encounter with the Messiah. She shared her testimony, others listened and responded, and her story had nothing to do with her résumé.

> Many Samaritans from that town believed in him because of the woman's testimony, "He told me all that I ever did."
> —John 4:39 ESV

Friends, our journeys may be different, but our God who helps us is the same. Some experiences result in deep, painful scars. But we should not hide our scars; they're meant to be cherished, respected, and shared. Our scars are our stories. Our stories are our victories. Our victories are our testimonies. Our testimonies lead others to the One who heals our wounds. God never wastes our pain. The precise reason God called each of us into the ministry of speaking and writing is to lead others to Jesus. We all need a reminder of who gives us both hope and help.

One of the most effective ways of doing so is through our experiences. "And if someone asks about your hope as a believer, always be ready to explain it" (1 Peter 3:15 NLT).

When we stand before our Father in heaven, I don't think God will care if we attended seminary or not. I believe God will delight and rejoice, knowing we shared Jesus with others!

NEXT STEPS:

Write out your testimony. Now let's take a deep breath and step out of our comfort zone. Share what you wrote with your safe group of kingdom warriors.

GOD'S PEACE WITHIN US

LAURA McPHERSON

I am leaving you with a gift—peace of mind and heart. And the peace I give is a gift the world cannot give. So don't be troubled or afraid.

—John 14:27 NLT

Our hearts desire peace, but we live with a great deal of uncertainty, chaos, and unrest.

We believe peace is what we experience when life seems perfect, or there is a lack of conflict, trouble, or financial struggles.

As writers, we may think peace is the certainty our material will be published or become a best seller. Perhaps peace will be ours when our platform is large enough, or we find the right agent and sign with the right publishing house.

But none of these things are within our control, and if we base our peace on them, we'll be disappointed. The blessing is this peace is not something we have to conjure up or look for. Peace is something we already have available within us through the Holy Spirit's presence.

In modern lingo, Jesus is telling us he has our back, and he equips us.

As humans, we look for peace in other places—vacations, spas, long walks, and an infinite list of other things. As writers, we look for peace in recognition, sales numbers, the right agent, or acceptance in the right groups.

These things allow us to access peace with greater ease, but they don't create peace.

Peace is internal—not external—and is a gift from God.

So, you might ask if having peace amid the rejections, looming deadlines, and blank pages is possible.

The answer is yes.

I like to visualize God's peace in my life with this illustration: I am lying on my back on a raft, floating down a river. It's a beautiful view. I'm looking at the sky, tree branches, and gorgeous cliffs overhead.

No matter what condition the river is in, God is asking me to relax, trust, and stay on the raft. He wants me to see the whole picture, the larger picture. That's why he wants me looking up.

What is true in our everyday life is also true in our writing life. Peace comes from God, not from our circumstances. God's peace and our desire for a trouble-free life are not connected.

Sometimes, when I experience discord, my first thought is I'm not trusting God. But when I look closer, I can see the truth. I've gotten too deep into the details. *Will the room be cold, will I have to wait a long time, will the procedure hurt, will I get the results right away, and many other thoughts.* I've narrowed my focus to the details and not the larger picture.

This is when I need a gentle reminder to look up and know God is in control—and he is in the details. What the world gives us is a far cry from what he gives us. With his peace, we don't have to conjure up anything. We don't have to figure out the specifics. We don't have to work so hard for peace.

Peace isn't the absence of something—bad reviews, blank pages, or back aches.

Peace is us embracing what we already have and allowing the calm to come through.

Believe God when he says, "For I know the plans I have for you, declares the Lord, plans to prosper you, not to harm you, plans to give you hope and a future" Jeremiah 29:11.

NEXT STEPS:

- Trust in the larger picture. God's got this.
- Get rid of *What if* and *If only* thinking. Live in the present circumstances.
- Live in gratitude.
- Breathe—God in, me out.
- Love and accept yourself.
- Evaluate your expectations.
- Let go of things and people that are out of your control.
- Pray.
- Meet with God every day.
- Take care of the mind, body, and soul.

In 1 John 4:4, God promises he is greater than our enemy. This promise allows us to believe there is a power greater than this world—one who will stand with us. How might you use this promise to overcome barriers or obstacles preventing you from accessing Christ's peace?

RELEASE THE PRESSURE

LESLIE THOMPSON

Whatever you do, work heartily, as for the Lord and not for men, knowing that from the Lord you will receive the inheritance as your reward. You are serving the Lord Christ.

—Colossians 3:23-24 ESV

As a writer, your vocation can be your ministry. Perhaps you write devotionals, Bible studies, Christian fiction, or praise-filled poetry. Using our craft for God's glory can be immensely fulfilling and keep us motivated to continue producing new work. But sometimes, the writing seems insufficient. We see others doing great things for the kingdom—they teach Sunday school classes, serve on mission trips, share tracts on street corners, or open orphanages overseas—and without warning, we feel our writing carries little weight. The voice in our head says, "You're sitting in front of your laptop while others are bringing sacks of food to the poor in remote villages. You don't have a ministry. You have a niche."

Friend, that is a lie from the pit of hell.

The enemy tries to convince us we are not enough, and what we do doesn't make a difference. Likewise, legalistic people may argue if we're not active and engaged in mission work or evangelism, we're not making an impact for God's kingdom. Our Father says something different. "For we are God's fellow workers. You are God's field, God's building" (1 Corinthians 3:9 ESV).

The Father invites us to engage in his work with a willing heart and with joy wherever we are, whether as a parent, white-collar professional, hourly employee, or solopreneur. We can honor God as much in the marketplace as in the mission field because the two are the same. The apostle Paul was a tentmaker, and through his profession, he met Priscilla and Aquila, a Jewish couple who also made tents for a living (see Acts 18). They later accompanied him to Syria and helped believers in the emerging church at Ephesus—all because they met and developed a friendship with someone who worked in the same field.

Your writing can open doors, and your work can lead to meaningful relationships. Over time, everything we do can be ministry when we let Jesus lead the way. Every place we set our feet becomes holy ground when we purpose to shine the light of Christ in our walk. Every word on the page becomes a point of connection with God as our heart aligns with his. Yes, your writing is your ministry because you are using the gifts and talents God gave you in the forum he placed you. You are not limited to ministry through the written word, but your work carries weight and makes a difference. A big difference.

When we write, we can leave a lasting impression. We can reach a broader audience than we know. How many times have you forwarded an article you found useful or passed along a favorite book to a friend? Others may be sharing your work behind the scenes or reading once again something you penned for renewed encouragement in a difficult season. Believe God will get your words in the right hands to accomplish his purposes. As long as we are faithful to continue in our craft, we can trust God will put our work in front of those he meant to read our message.

Remember, too, you don't need to pen a best seller to make a profound impact. We see books from Christian communicators, pastors, and Bible teachers at the top of the Amazon rankings. Doubt may surface about your work because your audience is small. But what if your story keeps one person from suicide? What if your blog post ignites faith in an atheist and leads them to salvation in Christ Jesus? What if your article on biblically based financial principles helps a young couple get a handle on their money, put an end to their frequent fights, and heal their marriage? Is that not ministry? Is that not enough?

We may never know the impact of our work. What matters is to stay connected to our Creator and continue to share his love through our writing. Give yourself grace in the process and avoid comparing yourself to others. There is no pressure to perform, only the call to obedience from a heart of gratitude, as we shine the light of Christ in all we do.

NEXT STEPS:

Think about a written work that made a positive impact in your life. Perhaps a novel, blog post, or the lyrics to a song drew you in. Reread the piece, if possible, and reflect on how the words spoke to you. Then pray in faith and humility, asking the Father to bless your writing, so you can bring hope and healing to others, too.

HELP! I'VE GOT A NUMB BUM!

SHARON TEDFORD

Don't you realize that your body is the temple of the Holy Spirit, who lives in you and was given to you by God? You do not belong to yourself, for God bought you with a high price. So you must honor God with your body.

—1 Corinthians 6:19-20 NLT

We've all been there. The chair doesn't take long to lose the comfy-ness feel. We shift from one "cheek" to the other as our backsides go numb. We try to find a new, more comfortable spot and realize we've run out of square inches we haven't already sat upon for hours.

When we write, we get in the zone. We plow on. We let nothing stop us from pouring out onto the page when the word-well hits a literary spring. When we strike communication water, we let the stream flow.

While we enjoy experiencing times when the current of text is so fierce the words threaten to whisk us away, we may find we are heading toward the top of a rampant waterfall with craggy rocks below.

The realization hits: if we don't take a break and move our numb bums around a bit, then trouble is on the way.

Because when we fail to move, we move toward failure!

When I get stuck at my computer, my vision blurs, my back hurts, and I feel twitchy. Those discomforts are a message from my body that I need a break.

I hear the voice of reason loud and clear as my brain has become a bit disengaged from the task. If my body's not happy, my brain isn't either.

We want to honor God with our talents, but our tired, mistreated bodies make our intentions difficult. We can demonstrate great reverence to God in and through our work and relationships. Will we also display our full devotion, honoring him with a commitment to care for our bodies as well? I've had to find a new perspective.

Romans 12:1 tells us:

> And so, dear brothers and sisters, I plead with you to give your bodies to God because of all he has done for you. Let them be a living and holy sacrifice—the kind he will find acceptable.
> This is truly the way to worship him.

Paul had to plead with our brothers and sisters of old to look after their bodies. Lack of self-care is not a new problem created by our fast-paced cyber world. God's deep compassion for us has always extended to our physical health and how we steward our well-being. He knows when we pay attention to the "temples" he's put us in, our worship (in whatever form we use—writer, speaker, singer, or artist) will be deep and impactful.

This is not to shame you or cause you to feel guilty but to encourage you to think more deeply about how we worship our heavenly Father with our bodies as we write.

Have you ever considered pacing to be exercise? Well, it is. I had a pastor friend who had a literal groove in the carpet of his office. He found his best thoughts came as he walked, even if that was just up and down the length of his room while preparing his sermons. Movement doesn't have to stop the creative process; in fact, being in motion could even give our efforts legs ... so to speak.

Computer time plus blood-pumping time equals a more rounded application of this verse.

Will you join me today and determine to seek methods to get up and move about, even for a short time? Will you find ways to bless your body with increased oxygen levels and move more muscles than the muscles in those typing fingers?

NEXT STEPS: (PUN INTENDED!)

- Set a timer for twenty or thirty minutes. Put the timer on the other side of the room (or further if you like). When the timer sounds, walk across the room and move the switch to off. Repeat the process.
- Commit to having a lunch break. Stop for a length of time and include a variety of good, nutritious food, and commit to movement every day.
- If you have a staircase, purpose to walk up and down the stairs on the hour, every hour. (If walking or stairs are not an option for you, play a quick game of "head, shoulders, knees, and toes" from your chair.)
- Drink water! If you drink enough, you'll also have to get up once in a while, if you catch my drift.
- Have a dance break. Put on your favorite song and dance through the music!
- Listen to an audiobook of Scripture and walk around the room or yard.
- Walk in place and watch this fun YouTube channel as the host takes you on an adventure through nature in the comfort of your home. https://www.youtube.com/watch?v=Poku9EHPJOo

REMOVING THE STICKY

DONNA NABORS

My heart overflows with a pleasing theme; I address my verses to the king; my tongue is like the pen of a ready scribe.

—Psalm 45:1 ESV

Label the problem as writer's block. Perhaps I'm in a funk. Call it burnout, fatigue, loneliness, or laziness.

Sometimes I can't write because I have nothing to say. Well, my husband might not agree with this statement. But this feeling is not just about writing. Sometimes I don't want to volunteer at church or deal with people at work. Sometimes I just don't want to whatever.

I'm stuck, and the sticky feeling of being stuck is overwhelming.

Early one year, I gathered with writing friends for a weekend to review a course on goal setting. This was a great refresher for the goals I set the month before. We discussed having key motivators and triggers for each goal. I struggle with the proper motivation for my writing goals.

As a result of the weekend away, I decided to review my schedule at the beginning of each week and commit to realistic writing times. My full-time job and other commitments can make this difficult. Each week looks a little different.

With that in mind, I focused on my motivation to write. Why am I blogging, and why am I writing my next book? This is not just something I enjoy. God has asked me to do this.

The key motivator came without much delay. For each time I commit to writing during the week, I will remind myself of this one thing: God has asked me to do this.

Then I will ask a simple question: What is my answer today?

The best way to encourage someone to talk and share with us is to ask open-ended questions rather than yes and no questions. When you sit down to dinner and ask your spouse or children, "how was your day," they are likely to say "fine." A better question or statement might be, "tell me about your day," or "what was the best thing that happened today?" These are conversation starters.

On the other hand, when we talk about obedience to God, there is no discussion. This is yes or no. Will I, or won't I? Yes, a conversation might ensue like, "Yes, God. I'm tired, but I will obey. Please give me strength. Please refresh me during this time." But in the end, it's still yes or no.

If we set our goals with God's direction, I guess they could all include the following statement and question:

God has asked me to do this.

What is my answer today?

God has also shown me two reasons I get stuck and how to remove the sticky feeling.

First, I get stuck when I have nothing to give. I'm empty. In these times, I need to be filled. The result is like a crash diet—we lose our energy. Not that I have ever had to remind myself to eat. So maybe a better analogy is my car running out of gas or the battery dying. When there is no power source or fuel, the car is stuck. I don't think twice about eating, putting gas in the car, or recharging the battery when I need to. Why do I forget to recharge my spiritual fuel?

Second, I get stuck when I have plenty to give, but I don't. I become satisfied where I am and don't want anyone to mess up my safe comfort zone. I become fat and happy with life, and I get stuck.

I can fill up on what God has for me every day, or I can ignore him, sit idle, and become empty over time. I can also fill up on what God has for me every day and keep everything for myself until I can't receive any more.

The pattern becomes a vicious cycle—filling up just to turn off the flow and then run dry. I fill my car at the pump and turn off the pump when the tank is full. Sometimes I do the same in life.

The remedy is *filling up* and then, without delay, *pouring out.* I need a continual replenishment that energizes my words, feelings, commitments, and service. The words are there. The stickiness disappears. My fire is rekindled. My energy returns, and I can't be still.

The solution when I'm filled is to turn to others and pour into their lives. The fuel for my heart and soul will continue to pour in as I make room by pouring out to others. For writers, this means words on the page.

When I have nothing to say, I'm reminded to pour out, making room for more.

Lord, fill me up, then pour me out, and fill me up again. This is one repetition I don't want to miss.

NEXT STEPS:

Ask yourself these questions:
- What goals have you set that include obedience to God as the key motivator?
- What is your answer to what God has called you to write?
- Are you stuck?
- How will you commit to getting unstuck?

WRITE TIME WRITE NOW!

DEB DEARMOND

God's gifts and his call can never be withdrawn.
—Romans 11:29 NLT

I'm often asked, "Did you always want to be a writer and speaker?"

The answer is not simple. I believe I always felt the pull of God's Spirit to communicate with everyone around me. Just ask my teachers! Did I dream about writing and speaking as a professional? Nope. Did I aspire to write books and speak across the nation in ministry at this time in my life? Never!

As a child, I loved to read and looked forward to the Friday evenings Mom and I spent at the library. Words became important to me from a young age. And I *did* love to talk. My older brother used to roll his eyes when I engaged strangers in conversations. "Mom, can't you shut her up?" Mother smiled and shook her head.

I surprised no one when I landed in a career field that paid me to talk. For thirty-plus years, I owned a business providing executive coaching, training, and keynotes for small companies and corporate giants across the country and around the world.

Writing books never crossed my mind—although the thought crossed the mind of a few who knew me.

For twenty years, three people in my life routinely asked, "When are you going to write your book?" I hadn't a clue what they were talking about. When my husband asked, I recall thinking, *maybe he thinks if I write down my thoughts, the house might be quieter.* That didn't work out for him.

My brother was a journalist, and he, too, commented over the years, "You should be writing." I was puzzled. The only samples of my writing he'd ever read were the letters we'd exchanged during the last fifteen years of his life.

And then there was my stubborn friend, Eve. When I responded in frustration to yet another inquiry about writing a book, my answer was swift. "Eve! I'm happy. I love my career." Her reply was not what I expected.

She nodded, "Yes. But those are gifts God's given you. He's let you cut your teeth in the business world. But one day, dear friend, he will call those in for his kingdom."

"But writing is not what I do."

She grinned and said, "It's not what you *do*? Or it's not what you've *done*? There's a difference, you know. I dare you to ask the Lord."

Lightning bolt. One I could no longer ignore.

But write books? What would I write about? And who on earth would want to read them?

Yet nine years later, I've sold six books to Christian publishing companies and written over two hundred published articles in print and online. For eight years, I've written a regular column each month for a respected, international Christian magazine.

How did that happen? What changed? *God asked me to write.*

Acceptance wasn't overnight, but I sensed God's nudge to write. And when I obeyed, I experienced his sweet Spirit in a way I'd never known. Time at the keyboards became time with him. When I prayed for direction, God supplied.

"Write what you know" is advice offered to those with the desire. Turns out, that was the Lord's advice too.

So I wrote about relationships, communication, and conflict resolution. Eve was right. The topics and skills familiar to me for years in the boardroom became those the Lord asked me to invest in ministry. The focus was new—no longer business, but life in Christ—family, marriage, parenting, and grandparenting. All at once, God's plan all made sense.

I'm grateful for God's call on my life and overwhelmed by the hand he extended as I stepped into what I think of as my destiny. On occasion, people ask if I'm sad I was past midlife before I began to write. Not at all. The areas God directed me to required years of living and walking with Jesus through challenges in my role as wife, mother, sister, and friend.

One sweet joy of this experience is the chance to help others who might be feeling the same nudge. Supporting others as a writing coach has become my passion. I find the work rewarding, and I love to help writers through challenges. The opportunity to help them as they grow and transition into new opportunities is fulfilling.

Writing is a solitary activity and can be difficult. The industry is tough and can be discouraging. Some struggle with isolation. Others give up before they get started and abandon God's call. Their wonderful stories are lost, their mission unfulfilled.

Romans 11:29 is a powerful reminder: "For God's gifts and his call can never be withdrawn" (NLT). The love of words God placed in me as a child was *on purpose*, for *his purpose*, now. Perhaps, that's you, too.

For those who feel the nudge as you read this, don't ignore that prompt. You may be stunned by what God has in mind for you. Remember, the Lord never gives up on what he's called you to do. As I always say … it's never too late to finish, and it's always too early to quit!

NEXT STEPS:

- Do you doubt your ability to write? What brings the feeling to mind?
- How will you maintain an awareness of your call? Who will you ask who can support and encourage you in difficult times?

THE MIRROR OFTEN LIES

SHARON TEDFORD

For in Christ lives all the fullness of God in a human body. So you also are complete through your union with Christ, who is the head over every ruler and authority ... You were dead because of your sins and because your sinful nature was not yet cut away. Then God made you alive with Christ, for he forgave all our sins. He canceled the record of the charges against us, by nailing them to the cross. In this way, he disarmed the spiritual rulers and authorities. He shamed them publicly by his victory over them on the cross.

—Colossians 2:9-10, 13-15 NLT

Imposter syndrome is a universal ailment many people including writers experience at least once in their lives. If you've somehow avoided this nuisance, I salute you!

Months ago, as I wrote a song about stillness before God, a voice in my head said, "You don't know what stillness is! How can you tell others to wait for God when you're so impatient?" Then there was the time I wrote an article about how to rise up in faith. "Well, you may find writing about faith easy to do. But do you live a constant faith-filled life? If they knew what went on in your head, no one would ever pay attention to you."

Friend, that was the familiar voice of Mr. Imposter Syndrome, and sometimes his voice sounds much like our own. As we look at our reflections in the mirror, he spouts his lousy, loud lies. He is no gentleman, and we need to know how to show him the door!

When we breathe life into the doubts and fears rattling in our psyches and listen to Mr. S. (Mr. S. can refer to both Mr. Syndrome and Satan—two voices we must ignore), we give life to our enemy. Now is the time we nail this one down and learn how to kick such destructive thought patterns to the curb. I'm sure you've experienced the undesirable power of Mr. I. Syndrome from time to time. He's a timewaster, a brain-space squeezer, and an all-around unwelcome gossiper.

For me, he becomes active when I look in the mirror, and I find more "me" than just the skin I'm in. I see down to my core. I picture my soul and the imperfections there. I am always a party to my internal voice as she mutters a complaint, while the smile on my face declares all to be well. I perceive my inner turmoil as I fight to be kind when I want to yell and complain. I am always a witness to my tendency to hide from the world and not bother with the difficult task of evangelism.

You too? Of course.

Satan's greatest desire is to "steal and kill and destroy" (John 10:10). When he gets me to do his destructive work for him, he achieves his goal with no effort.

Should we be honest about our struggles? Yes! Ask the Lord for forgiveness. But, when I *berate* the reflection in the mirror, I'm not doing God's work; I'm doing the enemy's work.

We are complete in Christ because of the work he did on the cross. Jesus made us one with him. We are his children and comprehensively forgiven. As we walk with Christ, we are fully included in the kingdom of God because of the grace and mercy we have received.

Full grace. Complete forgiveness. We belong to God. And we should land right there.

When God's call deafens us, his words flow through us. When obedience drives us, we complete the projects. When faith steps in, we complete the chapters.

And now, let's be aware, for the fallen one's next step is to use his filthy tactics and try one last-ditch attempt to thwart what God has invited us to share. This is how he uses our hearts to stir our belief in his lies.

Make no mistake, the final attack comes from behind familiar walls.

And friends, we're in charge of whether we continue to allow this to happen.

Go back and read the Scripture attached to this chapter. See if there's any ammunition there to contradict the deceptions the fallen one aims at you. We should be like Jesus and use Scripture's heavy veracity to dispute Satan's weak and flimsy slurs.

Remember who you are in Christ, recognize the gross whispers of the adversary, and walk in the freedom of truth.

NEXT STEPS:

Use the Scripture in this passage to write words of truth on a mirror you use often. Say these statements aloud. Remind yourself *these words are true.*

- I am one in Christ and complete in him.
- Jesus is head over me. I am fully submitted to him.
- I am alive in Christ.
- I am forgiven.
- Any charges against me have been canceled because of Jesus.
- Jesus has disarmed all spiritual rulers and authorities.

EVEN IF IT'S ONLY A STILL, SMALL VOICE

LORI ALTEBAUMER

"Go out and stand before me on the mountain," the LORD told him. And as Elijah stood there, the LORD passed by, and a mighty windstorm hit the mountain. It was such a terrible blast that the rocks were torn loose, but the LORD was not in the wind. After the wind there was an earthquake, but the LORD was not in the earthquake. And after the earthquake there was a fire, but the LORD was not in the fire. And after the fire there was the sound of a gentle whisper.

—1 Kings 19:11-12 NLT

Raw, honest confessions of a humble author ... I dream of the mountain top experience, standing before the Lord as my words go out like a strong wind to break apart the stony strongholds locking nonbelievers in the enemy's dungeon. I long for my writing to shake the foundations of doubters until the truth blinds them. I want the work of my hands to set the world on fire with a passion for the Lord.

And this is when I sense the overwhelming need for humility stir in my soul as the Holy Spirit says, *Oh really ...?* He then reminds me how futile my efforts to create anything resembling the above-mentioned acts of God are.

The only gift I bring to the page—the message God wants to share through my work—is my obedience. Breaking strongholds, shaking foundations, and setting the earth afire with a God-seeking passion is in his power, not mine.

My honor is God including me in fulfilling his purpose. Perhaps one day he'll say to me, "Go forth and stand on the mountain before the Lord." Maybe my novel will land on a bestsellers list. Maybe the book will change thousands of lives and grow God's kingdom. Perhaps the blog will go viral, touching hearts worldwide with the healing balm of God's truth.

But the odds suggest this might not happen. There's a greater chance my mountaintop moment will look more like *the gentle whisper* (see 1 Kings 19:12 NLT) sent to Elijah after the power of the wind, earthquake, and fire had passed by.

The question I must ask myself is, *am I okay with that?*

To which the only acceptable answer for a life claiming obedience to my Lord and Savior is "yes!" Anything less than a complete answer in the affirmative reflects a life not fully submitted to the Lord.

Now let me be honest, I would love for any of the above scenarios to happen. Bestsellers' lists and awards would be a sweet honor. Letters from readers whose lives changed as the result of my obedience to write would make my heart rise within me. My feet would set about hopping up and down in the Happy Dance—a dangerous move for someone my age.

And a dangerous spiritual move for a person of any age.

After all, this is not my mountain to dance on. I didn't form it.

Am I as content to be used as the still small voice of God?

Maybe my most powerful words won't be in the pages of the next great bestselling novel or the viral blog post sweeping the internet. I could include them in the heartfelt condolences I pen to a grieving friend. Perhaps in the sincere thanks for a kindness or the actions of a friend that might otherwise go unnoticed. Or, God willing, the short comment I leave on a post, offering encouragement or support, or an email to a stranger letting them know people appreciate their service. These simple acknowledgments carry God's gentle reminder to a soul who feels unseen.

I love the verse above. I'm reassured God's strength exists in far more than the mighty moments of achievement, acclaim, or world renown. He doesn't value the strong wind any more than the gentle whisper. He doesn't need the earthquake to accomplish his purposes.

All he needs is my willing and obedient heart—a humbled heart knows the joys and contentment of standing in the precise spot where he placed me.

NEXT STEPS:

Take a moment to list five ways you could be the still, small whisper of God in someone's life today. Who can you send a note of thanks or encouragement to? How can you communicate love and appreciation in some small way on social media?

Use your calendar or planner to challenge yourself in this as an everyday habit.

CAT GOT YOUR TONGUE?

BECKY CARPENTER

> We know, dear brothers and sisters, that God loves you and has chosen you to be his own people. For when we brought you the Good News, it was not only with words but also with power, for the Holy Spirit gave you full assurance that what we said was true.
> —1 Thessalonians 1:4-5 NLT

We are *abnormal* messengers!

Yep, I said it.

As Jesus followers, let's wear this descriptor loud and proud. After all, what is normal?

Don't ask Google; I already did. Normal means "as conforming to a standard, common, or ordinary."[1] Considering this, how in the world could we be ordinary and serve a supernatural, extraordinary God?

We can't ... so let's embrace being abnormal. Let's resist conforming to the world's standards. Let's refuse to be normal. Let's reject the idea God meant for us to be ordinary.

Has God ever placed a message on your heart only to have the words take a U-turn before exiting your mouth? In other words, did you check up before sharing? A handful of us may not experience this problem. In fact, we might need to zip our lips on occasion. Guilty! But we'll save that for another message.

When the urge to speak burns within us right before the cat grabs our tongue, our reluctance to speak out is often the work of the enemy recalling our insecurities. Guilty again! Yet, those are the precious moments when the Holy Spirit is speaking to us, so our response is as simple as one word.

Yield.

Yield to the nudging and allow the Holy Spirit to not only speak to us but through us. When the Holy Spirit takes the wheel, there should be no U-turns on this crazy good, faith-filled highway of life. No stop signs. Only yield.

When we allow the Holy Spirit to guide our tongue, the words drive straight into the hearts of others. He uses our willingness, our mouths, and our hands to carry his message exactly where his words need to go. God has already prepared specific individuals to receive personalized messages. We are simply the messengers.

Let's unpack some Scripture that can override our reluctance and give us the confidence to write and speak the words God has called us to share.

The apostle Paul, the original *abnormal messenger*, takes the pressure off when he shares his personal experiences. "For Christ didn't send me to baptize, but to preach the Good News—and not with clever speech, for fear the cross of Christ would lose its power" (1 Corinthians 1:17 NLT).

Jesus has chosen us not for our wisdom or eloquent speech (thank you, Jesus)! He chose us for our willingness to yield to the Holy Spirit's leading. By showing up for the assignment, we are walking in obedience. We leave the rest to the Holy Spirit.

Paul also says, "For when we brought you the Good News, it was not only with words but also with power, for the Holy Spirit gave you full assurance that what we said was true ..." (1 Thessalonians 1:5 NLT). Another great Scripture passage is when God said: "For it was I, the LORD your God, who rescued you from the land of Egypt. Open your mouth wide, and I will fill it with good things" (Psalm 81:10 NLT). God said I *will* fill it! I love how God gives us powerful Scriptures to speak truth over our insecurities. Our God will fill us with the right words we are to share. God is reminding us in these passages, he will speak through us.

As followers of Jesus, being an abnormal messenger is recognizing the Holy Spirit living within us and allowing his power to manifest. Yielding to the Holy Spirit is what makes us different. As messengers for Jesus, we live, look, act, and react in different ways than others. After all, we are not of *this* world. We don't live according to the flesh. We live according to the Spirit (see Romans 8). We have the Holy Spirit hanging out with us, giving us all we need to speak God's truths in boldness and with divine confidence. "I, the LORD, have called you to demonstrate my righteousness. I will take you by the hand and guard you, and I will give you to my people, Israel, as a symbol of my covenant with them. And you will be a light to guide the nations" (Isaiah 42:6 NLT).

God gives us an assignment according to his purpose and will. Therefore, get ready for God to use you in a mighty way!

Friends, we are a light to the nations, which means Satan will attempt to impede our thoughts to detour our mission. This causes the cat to grab our tongues ... or our pens. It's time we slap the cat (not in a literal way)! Don't be silenced.

Yield and allow his light to shine through. His word is a light for our paths (see Psalm 119:105). The light of Jesus guides those words onto the exit ramp of our mouths and into the hearts of others.

His word is a contagious light capable of changing the world, but only when we share it.

NEXT STEPS:

Read, write out, and meditate on 2 Corinthians 5:20, Psalm 81:10, and Revelation 2:17. What is the Holy Spirit confirming for you in these passages?

FLATFORM PLATFORM

MICHELE McCARTHY

And I am sure of this, that he who began a good work in you will bring it to completion at the day of Jesus Christ.
—Philippians 1:6 ESV

I believed I was called to write a book.

One. Simple. Little. Book.

Who knew writing demanded multi-faceted rules? Correct font and font size, margin requirements, and ever-changing punctuation rules. The process of redline, write, and rewrite drew near.

I didn't know what I didn't know until I attended a conference for writers and speakers. One weekend at AWSA (Advanced Writers and Speakers Association), a protégé sliced my brain into a dozen plates. I felt an urgent need to keep them spinning in the air. Show don't tell, audience acquisition, social media, and platform number needs whirled nonstop.

Blog. Website. Twitter. Oh my.

My return home from said conference required not only the need to unpack my luggage but to off-load brain strain. Can you say *overwhelming*? I began to grasp where I stood. My platform was a flatform. Flat, as in horizontal. As in level with the horizon. As in zero, nada, zilch. Those people I needed to reach, the audience I must impact, the hundreds who will buy my book were not even a blip on my radar. No people knew they were my people. No people knew I would publish a book they must read.

I'd never penned a blog, put a face on Facebook, or tweeted a Tweet. Yikes.

I sit at my computer to write, in my own world, isolated from the public. Feels like home and deep comfort. Can you say *introvert*? Marketing my work seemed un-Christlike. Merchandising feels, well, prideful and scary.

Welcome to the flatform platform club. Moses and Peter must have been early members. Moses's attempt to free his Hebrew brothers near the palace failed. He was pasturing a flock of sheep in the wilderness when God called him to free his people in Egypt. His assignment required he speak to Pharaoh. Moses didn't want to speak. He didn't feel eloquent. He didn't want a platform, even with God's provision. He argued with God over his qualifications. Flatform platform Moses was soon to be a household name.

My own messages may not deliver Israelites, but when God gives me a message to share, a platform is necessary. Thank goodness God is in the business to equip. With God's guidance, this computer illiterate built a website, published a blog, and wrote a newsletter. One step at a time, I inflated my flatform and rode my thin raft across the Red Sea with God's guiding rod in my hand.

Peter liked to talk. He wasn't afraid to blurt out what others in the room wanted to say but were afraid to voice. God inflated Peter's flatform into a platform for the kingdom. Peter didn't resist speaking as Moses did, but he needed God's guidance just the same.

God is the platform builder. Jesus enveloped Peter with forgiveness for his three denials and commanded him to feed his sheep. God empowered Peter with the Holy Spirit in Acts 2 to speak to the multitude and guide his powerful influence on his audience. God's breath enabled Peter's platform which still ministers to millions today.

Has my audience or my email list achieved massive numbers? No. Unflattening a platform takes time. Book promotion and gathering an audience is a process. Airing up a flatform requires the breath of God. He opens the doors. He is our promoter. I listen close for the wind of his voice to direct my next step. Moses and Peter, infused with God's power, spoke God's truth in boldness. God expects no less from us. If the Lord gives us a message to articulate, he will equip us.

As we fill our lungs with the breath of God's direction and provision, we will see our flatform stretch, widen, and balloon into the platform God has for us.

NEXT STEPS:

If you have not done so already, build your website. Many options are available. You can build your own or hire a website builder. Ask the Lord to show you which direction you should take today.

SETTLE DOWN

LAURA MCPHERSON

> Humble yourselves, therefore, under the mighty hand of God so that at the proper time he may exalt you, casting all your anxieties on him, because he cares for you. Be sober-minded; be watchful. Your adversary the devil prowls around like a roaring lion, seeking someone to devour. Resist him, firm in your faith, knowing that the same kinds of suffering are being experienced by your brotherhood throughout the world. And after you have suffered a little while, the God of all grace, who has called you to his eternal glory in Christ, will himself restore, confirm, strengthen, and establish you.
>
> —1 Peter 5:6-10 ESV

Many of us have experienced nudges, quotes, Scripture, and outright messages encouraging us to write. The messages resonate with us, and we ask: Am I called to write? Write what? Do I have a story or theme? Am I called to write something I need to research? What would that be? Am I called to write something to others? Am I capable of doing this? So many questions ... several without obvious answers.

How do we know we're called to write? If I could answer the question with certainty, I might end up rich. Rich in money? Perhaps, but of greater value, rich in connection and relationships.

Several years ago, I was encouraged to write a book. At the time, I served as a speaker to various groups. I found my greatest encouragement came when I wrote and taught a Bible study for young moms. As much as I enjoyed the experience, I questioned whether my material was "good enough" for a book.

When I decided to go ahead and write the book on the material I was teaching, a variety of messages swam through my mind. This included freestyle swimmers who flowed through the process without effort. Others were breaststroke swimmers who appeared to be laboring as they reached their goal. Then there were smooth backstroke swimmers who pushed through but got off course here and there.

I'd like to tell you my decision to write the book went swimmingly well. Overall, things worked out, but each lesson had challenges. I faced deadlines. I wondered if my work was scripturally sound. I hoped my subjects and illustrations were interesting, and I questioned whether the homework was on track. I was concerned about whether my teaching was effective. Bottom line, I let my tendency to overthink take hold.

Through all this speculation and overthinking, God impressed upon me to ask friends for prayer to include both the young moms and me. He also reminded me I needed to be fed and continue with my quiet time and spiritual growth. He arranged for people and events to remind me of my need for humility and vulnerability. There were times I knew I took shortcuts in my preparation, so I never felt settled as I approached each meeting. God helped me settle down by trusting him and his words in 1 Peter 5:6-10.

How do we settle down when our anxious thoughts keep intruding, even with the good ideas that could be useful? They come when we're driving, watching television, or as we try to fall asleep. New ideas can happen anywhere and anytime. Even useful thoughts can create anxiety.

Our thoughts and words reside in our brains. The only way to control them is to manage our thought processes. What works for me is to practice talking to my brain. "Don't go there, girl." Or I quote Scripture out loud to fit the situation. Equip yourself with a motto or Scripture to help you settle down when you need peace of mind.

I would like to clarify feeling settled doesn't mean we don't have any concerns or worries. Feeling settled means, we can push through. God loves and cares for us. He is our greatest encourager. Each day, use wisdom and ask him to order your day and protect you from the thoughts the enemy throws at us.

Below are additional strategies to help us refocus, feel calm, and settle down:

- Go for a walk. Read a book. Watch a comedy
- Write in your journal. Work on a jigsaw puzzle.
- Cook. Exercise. Paint. Call a friend.
- Don't over plan or over-commit. Take time for reflection and prayer.

NEXT STEPS:

If you're interested in gaining support as a writer during stressful times, you have many options.

- Attend a writer's conference.
- Join a writer's and or speaker's group who will support and navigate this journey with you. If you can't find a group in your vicinity, find one online.
- Join a reputable writers/speakers national association.
- Take one day at a time. Settle down and remember, there is always tomorrow.

DRINKING SAND FROM THE WELL

SHARON TEDFORD

Jesus replied, "If you only knew the gift God has for
you and who you are speaking to, you would ask me,
and I would give you living water."
—John 4:10 NLT

No matter how long I stared at the computer screen, I
couldn't make the words appear. My think tank was toast.
My prose packet was parched. My sentence supply had
seized.

What now? How was I supposed to spur people on with
encouragement when I was drained and empty?

For weeks, I had poured out encouragement to people.
I had written articles, given podcast interviews, taught
online, led worship, and taken part in group prayer times.
Each activity was a gift from God, and I loved every second.

But as I worked toward another project deadline, I was
disappointed to find my creativity was all gone. I had given
away every drop and felt like I was drinking sand from a well.

To hit the target date, I couldn't set the work aside for
another day when I felt in a creative mood. I had to write
now, regardless of the circumstances. I had started my day
with worship and Bible study, so I didn't understand why
I now found myself so thirsty. As I wandered around the

desert of the Blank Page, I felt there was no hope of escape. I had to find a way out.

Can you relate?

Although we may feel uncomfortable, this place of desperation is a great spot to land. When I realize my great need for my great God, I put myself right back where I need to be—sitting at his feet. I will pause and walk away from the screen for a few minutes. I lift my eyes and shift my focus off the work and onto him. I find refreshment in the balm of Scripture.

When we find our creativity river is as dry as a bone, then maybe we've "... abandoned ... the fountain of living water ..." (Jeremiah 2:13 NLT).

How should we quench our parched spirit?

First, let's open our Bibles. Find a favorite psalm or Scripture passage that fills you with hope. God's Word brings life and refreshment, even when our circumstances make us feel discouraged. When we allow God to speak to us through his powerful Word, he is sure to fill us. If we stop for a few minutes and refocus on our King, who gives us all things, he will help us capture those elusive words.

What else will help?

We should rest for a moment and chat with God. When we pause the frantic scramble for content in our brains and redirect our attention to the Lord, we will recalibrate our route. We must be single-minded in our pursuit of *him* first and put our quest for content in the proper place. When we do, he reminds us of his plan and reveals the path he's already plotted out for this piece of work.

When we do this, won't we find the adage, "let go and let God" rings true?

Another fantastic way to satiate our dry imagination is to immerse ourselves in a bath of worship music. Find a beloved hymn or modern praise song and be covered with tones of refreshment. The internet offers almost unlimited options of Christian. Pick one you love and plug your ears in!

ACCELERATE YOUR JOURNEY: WORKING WITH A WRITING COACH

DEB DEARMOND

Let the wise hear and increase in learning, and the one who understands obtain guidance.
—Proverbs 1:5 ESV

Writing a book had never been on my radar. Although I'd long been a bookworm, I considered myself a reader, not a writer. I was secure and happy in the business I'd built. The job was interesting and fulfilling, and I met wonderful folks across the globe.

I was fifty-five when I realized writing was more than an interesting possibility but a call on my life from the Lord. I was stunned. Overwhelmed but excited. And when I aligned my focus and time with his calling, the topic of the first book was apparent to me.

What was not apparent was how to make that happen.

As a voracious reader, I often found myself caught up in a story. I paid fleeting attention to the actual components of the craft. I hadn't noticed the importance of how the words on the page came together to create a wonderful manuscript. I knew from experience a gift from God was a good start. I believed the Lord would guide me in the process, and I'd learn what I needed to become an author.

But as is true for any of us whom God presses into tackling something new, more effort is required. I had to learn how to write—and how to write well. There is a major difference between the two.

My first steps toward writing were simple. I purchased several books on the craft of writing and attended a local writer's group. I never returned. I was the only nonfiction writer present that evening. And the critique session was overwhelming.

The process was clearly defined, and the members receiving evaluations that evening were nervous. They had good reason to be nervous. Let's just say the bloodshed and tears were enough to convince me I'd find another avenue to travel on my way to becoming an author.

A few months in, I learned of a conference for writers and speakers three hours away. I convinced a friend, also an aspiring author, to attend with me. The course was helpful, and I met several great women. Among them was a woman whose warm approach and "you can do this attitude" encouraged the group. Kathy served as a speaker in a few presentation segments.

From the moment she stepped into the presenter role, I was impressed with her experience and knowledge. Kathy shared stories of her writing journey and mentioned she worked with those interested in development. I didn't know anyone who worked with a writing coach, but I was convinced we could be a good match. I wondered if she might be available to coach me.

But by the time we completed the drive home, I questioned the idea. *Why would she want to work with a greenhorn like me? She probably has a waiting list a mile long.*

I tucked the idea away and continued to slog through the work on my own. Kathy's name popped into my mind several times. When I mentioned the idea to my husband, he encouraged me to reach out to her.

Surprise! She was available, her fee was reasonable, and she was free to begin within two weeks. She reviewed my work to date and identified my strengths and opportunities. She asked what resources I was currently using—the conversation was short. Tutorials, tips sheets, and more came flooding into my inbox. I used the information to correct my original pages. What a difference. Flow, tone, word selection, and more. Who knew? Kathy did.

In ninety days, she coached me through completing three sample chapters and a one-sheet to describe the book. When we set this goal, she was clear I'd need to focus and discipline my time to be successful. Deadlines set, deadlines met. We established the timing as I prepared for my first writer's conference in Denver. I felt confident in the work, but anxious about my amateur status—especially the pitch. Kathy stepped in.

We reviewed the listing of industry pros together. She knew publishing and the players well. Kathy guided me to the editors and agents interested in my genre and steered me to make the best selections. I received three requests for a full proposal and sample chapters. An agent reviewed my proposal and sample chapters, and I signed with her the following week. Within a few short months, I had a contract offer.

I am convinced the decision to work with Kathy accelerated my writing career. We remained a team once the contract was final, and she coached me through completing my manuscript.

Over the last eight years, I've been blessed to publish six books, including several award winners with solid traditional houses. My writing has expanded to include an eight-year column with Lifeway publishing in their monthly magazine, appearances on Focus on the Family, and more than three hundred published articles. These God-given opportunities still overwhelm me. I'm humbled beyond belief. I don't say this to boast—I have no illusion I did this on my own. I was blessed with two mentors. The Lord called and guided. Kathy coached and mentored.

One of the most exciting turn of events occurred three years ago when I completed my studies to become a certified writing coach.

The writing life has been a wild ride. Are you ready to push the pedal to the metal?

NEXT STEPS:

A qualified coach can help writers navigate the journey in a fraction of the time required to DIY. Their skill and industry knowledge can save you from discouraging dead ends.

Before you sign a coaching contract:

- Seek recommendations and do your homework.
- Have they been published? How many books?
- Are they industry-savvy?
- Do they offer a contract that states the services, hours, and requirements?

GARBAGE IN, GARBAGE OUT

LORI ALTEBAUMER

What you say flows from what is in your heart.
—Luke 6:45 NLT

Perfect prose ... empowering insights ... no one sits down to write a pile of rubbish. No one sets a goal to pen something ordinary or lackluster.

We may invest a great deal of thought and effort in establishing the right environment to create the ideal mood. We search for just the right chair, invest in helpful software, and purchase colored pens and scented candles. If we can master these things, then we can pour forth a stream of words worthy of the best sellers list—maybe even worthy of becoming a classic.

But we overlook that age-old adage: Garbage in, garbage out.

Scripture tells us out of the heart, the mouth speaks (Luke 6:45).

The same is true for what we write. What is in our hearts will find its way onto our page.

Still, we fill our heads the same way we stuff the kitchen junk drawer. You know the one everyone has filled with expired coupons, pens that don't write, and rubber bands so old they've got dry rot?

An athlete focused on the next competition trains with fastidious attention to the details of what he eats, how much rest he gets, and yes ... even what he thinks about. True competitors watch their diet with the fine-tuned scrutiny of a scientist. They have experienced the difference proper nourishment makes for the physical demands in meeting their objective. They're also aware performance suffers when their fuel supply is not balanced. They take care of their bodies, and when they're off, they know why.

They know garbage in will likely spell failure.

But not us writers. We sit down to a blank page, and if no words come, we blame writer's block. If we slog through a day just to get words on the page, aware they are worthy of the trashcan, we say the muse wasn't with us.

Seldom do we look back or within.

We are stubborn and refuse to acknowledge our predicament is the result of garbage in, garbage out.

How is our mental diet looking these days?

Professional athletes are diligent and intentional about what they put in their bodies. Writers, scribes, and wordsmiths must exercise the same level of intentional dedication if we want to write to the best of their abilities.

We are often reminded to take care of our physical bodies. Writing can be a stationary, stressful endeavor. Lost in our story, we snack without thinking and sit without a concept of how long we've been hunched over the keyboard. When something hurts, we know why. And if we're smart, we make a change.

But when we consider our brains, we believe that's a whole different animal. If our minds are not working, not producing what we want, we say the inspiration has left us. We remind ourselves writer's block is real. Or we didn't have the right scented candle. We can't find our favorite pen, or someone sat in our spot.

We never consider the late-night Netflix show we indulged in or the *harmless* gossip we listened to in the church prayer circle might be the culprit.

The list of external things we can find to blame for our lack of creativity or originality is creative and original. But let's leave our brains out of this.

We should be able to put whatever we want in and still crank out a brilliant masterpiece, right?

Wrong.

Whether it's a lunch date with Negative Nancy and Gossiping Gayle, the television show I would be embarrassed for anyone to know I watched, or that I binge-read *Fifty Shades of Grey*, the result is the same. Garbage in, garbage out.

In Psalm 101:3, King David promises to be faithful to God, saying: "I will refuse to look at anything vile and vulgar" (NLT).

As people chosen by God to write for his glory and kingdom, we should exhibit the same faithfulness David professed.

Before I place anything unholy before my eyes, I will ask what manner of output this will generate. How will my thoughts be stirred and influenced? How will my words be colored if this is what I give my brain to digest? If this—whatever I take in—becomes the fuel for my writing, how well will I run this race?

NEXT STEPS:

Identify the things that routinely capture your attention. Make an honest evaluation about the quality of writing output you would expect to come from this mindset. Do they fuel or inspire your creativity in a positive, God-honoring way? What can you replace them with to add power to your writing?

Identify the writers whose work you admire. Spend five or ten minutes reading their work each day before you sit down to write.

Make a list of books, blogs, podcasts, and activities to fuel your thoughts with positivity, clarity, inspiration, etc. Review this list whenever you are tempted to put garbage in, and remember, the result will be garbage out.

WRITE? RIGHT!

MICHELE MCCARTHY

And he said to him, "If now I have found favor in your eyes, then show me a sign that it is you who speak with me."

—Judges 6:17 ESV

I can behave like Gideon when I ask God for a sign. Gideon laid out a fleece and requested first the fleece would be wet with the early morning dew, and the ground would be dry. For another confirmation, Gideon asked for the fleece to be dry and the ground to be wet.

I too asked God to clarify if I heard the Lord correctly in his call to write. God never told Gideon he was wrong to ask for a sign. In fact, the Lord followed through on Gideon's request. Whew. Makes me feel better!

While I know we can always depend on God's Word, sometimes we need clarification in personal areas. *Write? Is this your call, or have I misunderstood?* I believe God knows our hearts and intentions when we are sincere. We want to follow his lead but need a little reassurance.

Obstacle after obstacle littered my path. I needed illumination of what I believed I heard—a call to write books. Over time, I noticed I commented in conversations with the word "right." I'd never recalled using "right" as a reply.

"We're glad to be going on vacation."

I'd respond, "Right."

"Brother Bob preached a powerful sermon."

I'd reply, "Right, right."

"Sure is hot these last few days."

I'd answer, "Right."

I can be a slow learner, but at last, the message in my answers hit me upside the head. I said "right," but I was repeating the sound, "write, write, write" over and over. Ad nauseam.

An amazing God wink. His humor astounds me. He and I play with words all the time. He is the master of the use of words. God's Word is replete with complicated stories with characters with similar names. I can't help but scratch my head. Rehoboam, king of Judah, side by side with Jeroboam, king of Israel. Balak, king of Moab, paired with Balaam, a sorcerer summoned by Balak. And Elijah, the prophet, teamed with Elisha, the prophet.

God gave us the Word. The Word is Jesus. To say words are important to our Father is an understatement. He revels in words, enjoys words, and entices by words. Names he chooses have meaning. The Lord compelled me to compose stories of the power of words, both in my book relating my personal journey and the children's book seeds he planted in my heart. Never underestimate how the Lord can communicate with you.

God communicated his answer to my question "write?" with the word "right."

Now what?

Put your fingers on the keyboard and pour your heart out. Cry out the words. Laugh out the words. Get your message on the blank page. Edits come later. Recognizing your call to articulate a message and follow-through is not a simple process.

Daunting? Check.

Challenging? Check.

Sacrifice? Check.

Fulfilling? Check.

Commitment to cross the finish line is a must. Reports claim at least 97 percent who begin a novel never finish.[1] On the other hand, self-publishing has produced some less than stellar finished works. Obligation to complete your task needs to be paired with excellence.

Jim Denney makes a good point in his article "The Holy Call of Writing: Are You Called to Write." Denney puts forth, "We don't write out of a desire for fame or to gratify our own egos. We write to serve Him. And if we did not write, we would feel we are disobeying Him." He continues, "If you approach writing as a holy calling, your life will be marked by two qualities: enthusiasm and inspiration ... you have a sense God lives and works through you, and every creative act you perform is a loving imitation of the nature and activity of God the Creator."[2]

When God calls you to write, expect a cost. Creation takes time, effort, and money—as you attend workshops, build websites, and create promotional materials. Was there ever a person in the Bible God called who didn't pay a price? God's prophets were ridiculed. His chosen faced trials. King David refused a field offered to him as a gift. He told Oman he would buy the field because he did not want to give offerings to the Lord that did not cost him anything.

While the call to write comes at a cost, the reward of writing is genuine. Creating is fulfilling. Words birthed from inspiration and grit on display gratify. A completed task brings great satisfaction. Any pain during the creative process is long forgotten once you hold your *baby* in your hands.

In the end, the cost of our created efforts is a loving sacrifice to our Lord and worth the price.

NEXT STEPS:

You must feel the call to write since you are reading this book. I encourage you to sit before the Lord and ask for guidance. Should you attend a writer's conference? Should you invest in online training? Do you need to start with a blog or newsletter? Let God guide your next move.

LEAVE A LEGACY

LAURA MCPHERSON

> I will open my mouth in a parable; I will utter dark sayings from of old, things that we have heard and known, that our fathers have told us. We will not hide them from their children, but tell to the coming generation the glorious deeds of the LORD, and his might, and the wonders that he has done.
>
> —Psalm 78:2-4 ESV

God created us with the ability to impact his world. How we walk out our faith and live our lives should leave a legacy both in our relationships and spiritual matters.

When I write, with God's help, I hope to make a God-honoring impact. I pray the words I use and the concepts I offer will glorify him. When we share part of ourselves, we leave a gift for the next generation. What we share through our writing is testimony to our family and future generations. What we write, what we speak, and how we act send strong messages. Are these messages sending invitations to go deeper into our faith and invite others to follow? Are we writing with our reader's hearts and eternities in mind?

We live in a complicated, sometimes, overwhelming world. We may ask ourselves *how can I reach my world?* The answer is in the word *my*. God designed all of us with the ability to impact the world closest and most personal to us. We know who and what comprises our sphere of influence. Family, friends, community, clients, and anyone God puts into my life is included in my reach. This is exciting but fodder for anxiety if we are unsure why and to whom we are writing. This anxiety may cause us to shrink back instead of stepping forward.

Who is your audience? What are your goals?

Some of the best manuscripts tell stories about ordinary people and their everyday lives. Abraham's story, and many others in the Bible, have been passed down through the generations. Are they about exceptional people? No. God uses ordinary people like you and me.

Whether they proclaim our victories or confess our struggles, our writing can glorify God. Why does he insist we write with the purpose of passing these truths on, not only to our generation but generations to come?

The Lord wants us to recognize, remember, and glorify him. He wants our words to encourage others. Ordinary people just like us wrote the Bible—and they still make an impact today. Our stories reflect God's presence in our lives and our relationship with him and others. Our legacy must include the account of our lives for future generations.

Remember the woman Jesus met at the well? Her story created curiosity, and the townspeople wanted to know more. Many came to believe in Jesus because of her testimony. She had no training, but she spoke with boldness. She didn't go to conferences or take classes. She shared her story without delay, which had a transforming effect on others' lives. She left a legacy—one passed down for centuries and is still changing lives today.

How do you leave a legacy through your writing?

- Think about what God has done for you—saved you, provided for you, and encouraged you.
- Find Scriptures and biblical stories you can share in your writings.

- Include information that reveals God's character in what you write: grace, faithfulness, mercy, love.
- Ask the Holy Spirit and other witnesses to share what God does to influence and help your writing. Don't over-spiritualize, and don't minimize—make your writing real.
- Remind yourself your calling is to experience God's love, protection, and transforming power and then be a witness to the experience ... your legacy.
- The enemy may claim your work is insufficient or worthless. Resist him.

As Christian authors, we are in touch with the human and spiritual elements. We are charged to share God's goodness and love and our passions. He meets us along the way and guides us where he wants us to go. The Lord equips us to write on his behalf. What a gift!

NEXT STEPS:

Observe and reflect on how your writing impacts the lives of others.

Does what we write give glory to God? Our words aren't about being good or right. Stories about mistakes may end up glorifying God—despite what we've done!

Do your words encourage others, relieve them, or offer hope?

WHEN WORDS FAIL

KAREN DEARMOND GARDNER

> I rejoice in your word like one who discovers a great
> treasure.
> —Psalm 119:162 NLT

A great idea dropped into my mind. Tingling with excitement, I planted myself in front of the computer, hands hovering over the keyboard. Anticipation flows as I type. As easily as the words come, the words go.

I sit. And sit. The cursor mocks me. Inspiration wains. The deadline looms.

Has this been your experience?

Disheartening, to say the least. We may even question whether the *great idea* was so great after all. Did we jump ahead of God? We may think the problem is with us. Perhaps we're not writers after all. We may doubt our call—which creates apprehension and anxiety.

But wait ...

What if the idea you have is good but may not be the *main* idea? Might this be part of a bigger story you can't see yet?

This happens to me on a regular basis. But one specific situation stands out.

I agreed to write an article in two days. Not a simple task for me. I was stuck on where to begin, and the readers were not my typical audience. How could I gain their interest? What would they want to read?

The directions I received allowed me to write on any subject, with one exception, a single request. *"Don't promote your book."* But I *was* permitted to select a topic for the article *from* my book. I used the opportunity to educate these readers. Excitement flowed as I dripped words onto the page. As sudden as the words began, they dried up like a pond in a drought.

Out of desperation, I searched the website where the article would appear. There I discovered the writer guidelines. The resource included a list of subjects of interest to their audience, and right away, I identified an appropriate fit. The words flowed once again.

What actions can you take to stop the endless cycle of type, delete, and repeat?

- Check the guidelines or ask yourself, What do they need to know about my topic even if there's no direct impact on them?
- Invite like-minded people to help you brainstorm ideas. In this chapter, I considered dumping the topic and writing something different. I brainstormed with another author, which shifted the direction of this chapter.
- Prayer is always a good place to start, perhaps your go-to already. God cares about your writing. After all, he's the one who called you to write so he won't leave you hanging.
- What if your idea needs to be fleshed out? The challenge may not be beginning the story. The issue may occur in the middle or the end. Sometimes we need to step out of our box of what we think we should write about.

The focus is about getting words on the paper, streaming your thoughts, and letting them flow. Let the words set, then edit. You may find clarity in a second look as new ideas come to you.

Need to change direction? Add a twist by writing about an *aspect* of a broader topic. What is one thing you want the reader to know? How did God shift you from where you were to where you are?

On occasion, you may have to scrap what you've written and start over. Tip: don't delete your words; they may be useful in the future. Save them for another article.

Sometimes, we look beyond what we think we're capable of and remember when God called us to write. Maybe for you, writing is second nature. You can't help but write. Or you may be the one who didn't know you could write until you were fifty-seven. I couldn't string three words together, much less write sentences, pages, and chapters.

When I struggle to capture thoughts and ideas on paper, I remember the *moment* he called me to write. If you're struggling to write:

Stop. Pause. Listen.

Stop what you're doing. Stop fighting to put words on the page.

Pause, take a deep breath, and slowly exhale. Do it again. Do you feel the tension leaving? Do you feel your mind clearing?

Listen to your heart. Can you hear God in your heartbeat? What is he saying?

NEXT STEPS:

Write about the first time you either felt compelled to write or when he called you to write. Let the words flow. Don't overthink what you're writing, and don't edit as you go. This isn't about perfection. This is about recalling why you started on this wild and crazy journey.

As you read, feel the emotions of *why* you write.

Let your fingers hover over your keyboard and create ideas through words, sentences, paragraphs, pages, and chapters.

And go one step further. When someone asks what you do, tell them, "I'm a writer."

YOUR STORY IS SIGNIFICANT

LESLIE THOMPSON

For we are his workmanship, created in Christ Jesus for good works, which God prepared beforehand, that we should walk in them.

—Ephesians 2:10 ESV

At a recent Christian writer's conference, I sat next to a gentleman with a powerful testimony. In the span of a dozen years, he had endured many hardships, from battling drug addiction to periods of homelessness, clinical depression, losing loved ones, and sustaining a debilitating injury days before starting a new job. Throughout everything, however, he kept his eyes on Jesus. Even during the most difficult and agonizing seasons of his life, he stood firm in faith and trusted God to not only lead him through the valley but also to use his witness to help others in their trials.

This gentleman has been documenting his journey and testimony of the Father's enduring grace on social media for several years, but he never considered himself a "writer." He likely has written as many words as several published authors attending the conference where we met, but he was skeptical about writing a book. He questioned whether his story could make a difference.

I thought about the many nameless individuals in the Bible whose stories have encouraged and equipped Christians for generations. Consider the woman with the issue of blood and her radical act of faith, which the book of Luke chronicled. She suffered for twelve years with an affliction that made her unclean in the eyes of society. Although she had spent all she had on physicians hoping to find a cure, she was only healed when, in desperation, she touched the hem of Jesus's garment. After confessing she was the one who had touched him among the crowds, Jesus said to her, "Daughter, your faith has made you well; go in peace" (Luke 8:48 ESV).

When a nameless Roman centurion pleaded for Jesus to help his paralyzed servant, who was suffering at his home far away, Jesus agreed to go and heal him. "But the centurion replied, 'Lord, I am not worthy to have you come under my roof, but only say the word, and my servant will be healed. For I too am a man under authority, with soldiers under me. And I say to one, "Go," and he goes, and to another, "Come," and he comes, and to my servant, "Do this," and he does it'" (Matthew 8:8-9 ESV). The Messiah marveled at the centurion's faith and called the soldier's conviction to the attention of the disciples who were with him. "And to the centurion Jesus said, 'Go; let it be done for you as you have believed.' And the servant was healed at that very moment" (Matthew 8:13 ESV).

Perhaps the most significant biblical illustration of the power of our testimony is the story of the woman at the well. In the heat of the day, hoping to go unnoticed, a Samaritan woman of ill repute went to draw water at Jacob's well. Jesus was waiting there and asked her for a drink. "The Samaritan woman said to him, 'How is it that you, a Jew, ask for a drink from me, a woman of Samaria?' (For Jews have no dealings with Samaritans.)" (John 4:9 ESV). The two engage in conversation, and Jesus offers her the living water he came to bring. But when he tells her to go call her husband, we learn she has been married five times and is living with a man who is not her spouse. But Jesus already knew. Astounded at his insight, she believes Jesus to be a prophet. As their conversation continues, he reveals he is the Messiah.

Jesus opened her spiritual eyes, and this woman who lived with deep shame and was considered a social outcast ran into town to share the good news. "Many Samaritans from that town believed in him because of the woman's testimony, "He told me all that I *ever* did'" (John 4:39 ESV). Her testimony set off a chain reaction in the local community as people came to encounter the Son of God for themselves. They, too, testified Jesus was the Christ, the Savior of the world.

We read books and blogs by Christian celebrities and may think we can't make an impact if we do not have a platform and a large following. But God has a purpose and plan for each of our lives and will put our written work in the right hands. He will arrange introductions and open doors of opportunity if this is his will. Our job is to be obedient to the call and share our testimony with courage for his glory.

NEXT STEPS:

Think of a time when Jesus came to your rescue. Perhaps you were going through a difficult transition, such as a job loss or divorce, and through Christ, you received emotional support or financial provision. Reflect on how your testimony might help someone in a similar situation and pray about submitting your story of faith to a Christian blog or devotional.

PERFECTION AND PROCRASTINATION: PARTNERS IN CRIME

DEB DEARMOND

Our great desire is that you will keep on loving others as long as life lasts, in order to make certain that what you hope for will come true.
—Hebrews 6:11 NLT

Every writer or published author has dabbled or delayed in their quest to finish a writing project. This truth may comfort you. All creatives experience this at one time or another—the flow is interrupted, and the words disappear. William Zinsser, the author of *On Writing Well,* says: "A writer will do anything to avoid the act of writing."[1]

You're not alone. Statistics reveal 95 percent of the population procrastinates at times, with 20 percent of the population identified by Dr. Tim Pychyl as *chronic procrastinators.*[2] The trend continues to rise.

The cost of procrastination as a writer is significant:

- Missed deadlines
- Missed opportunities (often related to previous missed deadlines)
- Stress and pressure to get something on the page when you are not "in the flow"

- Damage to your reputation and reliability when work is late or poorly completed because you delay until the last minute

Is it possible to change the behavior? *It is.*

Dr. Tim Pychyl, the author of *Solving the Procrastination Puzzle*, has done a tremendous job of research on the topic. The good doctor identified a set of triggers that make a task seem more averse—also defined as daunting, overwhelming, or unpleasant.[3] And when tasks create a sense of dread or overwhelm, it's easy to see why we put them off. Perfection and procrastination are partners in crime.

So let's experiment with a quick exercise. Recall something you're struggling with now in your writing. I believe you'll find your concerns among the characteristics Dr. Pychyl discovered that make a task procrastination worthy.

Here are his top five examples and how they *sound:*[4]

- Fear of the Unknown—"I don't know how to get started."
- The Task is Difficult—"I can't do this. It's too hard."
- The Task is Boring—"I thought writing was a creative process. This isn't fun!!"
- The Task is Ambiguous—"I'm totally confused— every expert says something different."
- The task is Unstructured/Feels Overwhelming— "Who am I kidding? I'm not a writer."

Why does the way the words sound matter? You hear the words—these assessments are what we're *telling ourselves about ourselves.* And damaging self-talk can convince us to quit. If you believe you are called to write, this can be devastating.

These five procrastination traps are common but not always the most common, especially among creatives— including writers. The most common trap among this group is often believed to be *perfectionism!*

How do we address the evil twins of perfection and procrastination? What can we do when they strike?

Maybe you had a mom like mine who taught me "anything worth doing is worth doing well." Her exhortation to excellence has often served me. At times, I've discovered I can also be hypercritical of myself if the outcome is not perfect *at the moment*. Perfectionism lobbies for everything to be perfect *now* and limits the definition of success to an unrealistic standard. As Zinsser points out, "Clear thinking becomes clear writing; one can't exist without the other."[5]

How does your awareness of "clear thinking" equip you to write when perfection isn't present on the page? Acknowledge you're stuck, distracted, or discouraged. Recognize when procrastination badgers you to write tomorrow, go shopping, or clean out your closet when you should be at the keyboard. Think clearly and redirect your efforts to more manageable or appealing activities that still support your writing!

Stop staring at the blank screen. Don't rewrite the opening paragraph ten times and trash the work. Turn your attention to other tasks:

- Research material for your book or article.
- Work on the proposal: research comps, select a format.
- Read a chapter in a craft book or research an online resource to fill a knowledge gap.
- Edit work completed previously.
- Listen to a podcast on writing to advance your knowledge.
- Brainstorm with a writing buddy. Don't have one? Find one!
- Or write—and disconnect from the procrastinator's prayer: "Please God, make it all perfect right now!"

Is that last one possible? Successful writers know perfection is elusive—not always easy to attain. Have you ever finished a late-night writing session, hit Save with great satisfaction, convinced the writing is brilliant, then awaken to discover the work is not brilliant at all? Maybe not even passable. That's why there are second drafts, critique groups, and amazing lightning bolts when you are engaged with another activity.

NEXT STEPS:

Redeem the day—invest in dumping perfectionistic thinking in your writing. Pump your productivity with other writing-related tasks. Then return when you can think and write clearly.

And never forget—one can't exist without the other!

CONCLUSION:
IT TAKES A VILLAGE

BECKY CARPENTER

> Let us think of ways to motivate one another to acts of love and good works. And let us not neglect our meeting together, as some people do, but encourage one another, especially now that the day of his return is drawing near.
>
> —Hebrews 10:24-25 NLT

Get yourself a tribe; you'll be glad you did!

This statement should be an infomercial to promote all you brave messengers who jump to the front lines of the writing battlefield. I didn't realize there *was* a battlefield … until I said yes when God called.

Deciding to write for Jesus is easy. The actual writing is scary.

The first time I put my heart on a page for others to read, I felt I was clothed in plastic wrap. In other words, I felt naked. I experienced a level of transparency that exposed the secret spaces … no longer hidden, revealed for all the world to see.

Have you felt exposed and vulnerable in your writing journey? If so, you're right where God wants you. The good news is—you're not naked! Jesus has you covered! "I am overwhelmed with joy in the LORD my God! For he has dressed me with the clothing of salvation and draped me in a robe of righteousness. I am like a bridegroom dressed for his wedding or a bride with her jewels" (Isaiah 61:10 NLT).

Vulnerability elevates our discomfort. When we're uncomfortable, we lean in. When we lean in, we listen. When we listen, we learn. When we learn, we grow. Vulnerability invites our comfort zone to be stretched right into God's will. We become dependent on the Father's help. His help produces an outcome that lands in the center of His will. "For I hold you by your right hand. I, the LORD your God. And I say to you, 'Don't be afraid. I am here to help you'" (Isaiah 41:13 NLT).

God helps us in so many ways. He can even send us a personalized support group. God not only loves people—God loves *through* people.

God knew I needed reinforcements. He knew I needed others who have already braved the battles of insecurities and challenges of writing for a higher purpose. In God's gracious timing, incredible women of God who love Jesus and love the art and purpose of writing surrounded me. God sent me my tribe.

As writers, isolating ourselves is easy as we get lost in our writing assignments. In the busyness of our calendars, we're tempted to cancel social commitments and interactions as we marry ourselves to our thoughts and keyboards. By God's design, we are to reside in a community with others, especially as we work together as kingdom builders.

> May God, who gives this patience and encouragement, help you live in complete harmony with each other, as is fitting for followers of Christ Jesus. Then all of you can join together with one voice, giving praise and glory to God, the Father of our Lord Jesus Christ.
>
> —Romans 15:5-6 NLT

Jesus had his own intimate support team. His tribe started with twelve. His personal village of cheerleaders who absorbed his teaching as they walked with him. They shared in his victories—and his sorrows.

Throughout the gospels, the disciples traveled and ministered alongside one another, all working together, sharing the love and mission of Jesus.

When God calls, God equips. He orchestrates divine connections. He places appointed individuals in our path to encourage us and hold us accountable. This is our village. Our tribe—the individuals God has handpicked to walk alongside us throughout our kingdom assignments. When God's hand is in our relationships, the bond is elevated. Your tribe will become far more than a support group. They are your team of cheerleaders and prayer warriors. "Brothers and sisters, we urge you to warn those who are lazy. Encourage those who are timid. Take tender care of those who are weak. Be patient with everyone" (1 Thessalonians 5:14 NLT).

Your tribe becomes a safe space of joined hearts who share struggles and celebrate victories. Your tribe stretches you and strengthens you. In other words, they are *your people*. This group is far more than your village; they are your forever friends. "As iron sharpens iron, so a friend sharpens a friend" (Proverbs 27:17 NLT).

I'm sure thankful for my tribe. You've met them throughout the pages of this book.

NEXT STEPS:

Pray with intention about your writer's tribe. Connect with online writer's groups and attend professional writer's conferences. This is where you will find your people.

Inspired to create a tribe of your own? The resource pages following this final chapter are an amalgam of the tips, tools, and practices from the women of Living Write Texas.

AUTHOR BIOS

Becky Carpenter is an international speaker, writer, teacher, and missionary. She is the founder of *One Day Closer Ministries* and has spoken at more than one hundred forty events. She is a blogger, Bible study contributor, and frequent podcast guest. Becky is working on her first book, *One Day Closer*. BeckyCarpenter.net (Speaker website) Onedaycloser.net (Ministry website)

Deb DeArmond is an award-winning author and certified writing coach. Her books cover marriage, family, and Christian life. *Bumper Sticker Be-Attitudes* is a humor-tinged look at life, and *We May Be Done But We're Not Finished* covers living large after fifty. Deb has published more than three hundred articles and writes a monthly column for *Lifeway's Mature Living Magazine*. Connect with Deb on her website debdearmond.com.

Donna Nabors points women to find hope in God's Word. Donna has authored three books: *Pearls: 5 Essentials for a Richer Prayer Life, Shattered Dreams to Treasured Truths: Transforming Life's Disappointments*, and *Treasured Truths,* a devotional companion. Donna contributed to AWSA's book *Arise to Peace* and is published in *Spark Flash Fiction*. She blogs at donnanabors.com.

Karen DeArmond Gardner's first book, *Hope for Healing from Domestic Abuse*, was published in 2021 by

Kregel Publications. She is the Founder of *Another One Free* for domestic abuse survivors and is a certified trauma advocate. A frequent podcast and interviewee, you can connect with Karen at her website AnotherOneFree.com.

Laura McPherson, MS, LMFT, is in private practice in Kingwood, Texas. She has served as a speaker for twenty years on topics related to her specialties and guides those who desire to make healthy changes in their life. Her first book, *It's Me, Not You: Key to Healthy Relationships,* was released in 2021 by EABooks Publishing

Leslie J. Thompson is an accomplished freelance writer and former magazine publisher, with more than twenty-five years' experience. She holds a master's in journalism from NYU and has contributed to numerous national and regional magazines. She also shares stories of God's work in her life on her blog at outoftheherd.com.

Lori Altebaumer writes across several genres. She won the 2019 Foundation Award for her short story, *Home*, from the Blue Ridge Mountain Christian Writer's Conference. She was a 2020 finalist for two Selah Awards and Director's Choice Award for her novel, *A Firm Place to Stand* from Blue Ridge. The book also placed third for the AWSA Golden Scrolls.

Michele McCarthy is a Texas Christian University graduate, author, and speaker. She's an AWSA member and author of *Shattered, Stirred and Shaken*, her personal testimony. Her two award-winning children's books include *Aunt Ida Clare* (First place winner of the 2021 Golden Scrolls) and *Aunt Ima Mazing*. For more information: michelemccarthybooks.com

Sharon Tedford is a British-born international singer/songwriter, author, and host of the award-winning podcast, *God in the Ordinary*. She released her first book and album both entitled, *Stand* in 2017. Sharon was a contributor to *Arise to Peace* from AWSA in 2021. Her forthcoming children's book was a Cascade Oregon Christian Writer's contest finalist in 2021. Sharon is also a popular speaker and watercolor artist.

BUILD A TRIBE OF YOUR OWN

Deb DeArmond, Managing Editor

Our members are often asked, "How did your group come together? And what are you doing to maintain the enthusiasm and commitment that's lasted three-plus years?" So, we thought we'd share a bit of our story in the event perhaps you, too, are hoping to create a supportive tribe of writers.

Living Write Texas began with a serendipitous connection between three Texas women who met in Nashville at a writer's conference in 2018. We dined together on the final evening and promised to stay in touch.

Within a few months, we met for lunch, and our conversation turned into a discussion concerning the total lack of writing groups in our area. We agreed we would be thrilled if someone started one in the Dallas-Fort Worth area.

Michele glanced in my direction. "You could start one, Deb. You've been writing for five years and have three published books. There's so much you could teach others."

Laura joined the chorus, and within minutes we sketched out the possibilities.

But where and how would we find the right women to join us?

God quickly answered this question. Within three short months, we held our first weekend retreat. Ten women arrived at a beautiful home on the shores of Lake Worth. The property belonged to Michele's generous son, who made the house available.

We arrived late Friday afternoon and planned to depart on Sunday afternoon at two o'clock. None of us knew everyone this first time around, which is a bit scary in retrospect. I knew Sharon, who invited Leslie. I also knew Donna, who brought us Lori. Rene and Karen were friends who desired to write, and they came along, too. Karen invited Michelle number two, and we were off and running.

We opened our time together with worship. Sharon, a talented musician and recording artist, led us to the throne as the music washed over us. Any nervous concern or uncertainty vanished. Everyone received a set of prompts before the retreat. The directions requested each attendee to select a prompt and write a short story to share the first night. As each read their work, we gained glimpses of the personality, heart, and writing gifts assembled.

We invested the next day and a half in additional topics of interest, but most pressing was the discussion I'll title "What Now?"

We explored ideas and revealed personal areas of knowledge we could share and topics of interest to explore. We decided to meet three times each year and established a set of dates for the remainder of the calendar. Three years later, we're still showing up, grateful for this gathering of women.

Two of our original members departed as they discovered they enjoyed writing, but it was not their primary focus. We filled one spot but feel no pressure to fill the other. God will let us know when the time is right. We've limited membership to ten.

We learned several lessons in our first few retreats and adjusted along the way. So we've created a list of the factors we believe have forged a unique and successful writing group.

- Worship. Hands down, this was mentioned most often. We continue to worship as the opening activity of the first night and again each morning. In those moments, we're reminded we write for the Lord, which allows us to begin with open hearts. You may not have a musician in your midst who can help create this atmosphere. Use recorded music and sing along. A quick search online provides multiple options—many with the lyrics scrolling on the screen.

- Writing Prompts. We have laughed and cried over the incredible works offered during this time. It reminds us there's more than a single mandated route to create wonderful stories. The group's diversity in style, voice, and approach expands our insights on writing as well. You will find books filled with these story starters available online.

- Structure. The format of each retreat remains close to our original gathering. There is always an agenda to help narrow our focus and manage the time. Our coordinator queries the group on topics they'd like to hear or present. Our members are a well-informed force. Each seems to have a specialty: social media, craft, publishing, marketing, websites, blogging, newsletters, and articles. These micro-courses provide great tips and tools to expand our knowledge. And if we need a topic without a resident expert among us, members volunteer to research and bring the findings to the team.

Once a possible agenda emerges, our coordinator seeks feedback from the group. On occasion, we will schedule a Zoom call to confirm or correct the agenda or discuss other related business.

- Leadership. A ship with no captain flounders. From the beginning, Deb was the rudder that kept us moving full speed ahead. As the group matured in relationship, knowledge, and experience, others needed to assume leadership responsibilities. Some believed they were not ready or equipped for the role but stepped up. If this is your situation, mentor, train, and prepare others to take the lead as needed for an event, retreat, or group project. With three years together, everyone in this group is capable of leading—and they do!

- Prayer. We make prayer a component of every retreat. We ask for God's blessing on our time together and remind us he is the center of all we do. But it doesn't end there. We pray for one another whenever the need arises by email, messenger, or phone. Concerns for family, writing challenges, health, and more. We've grown together over the years, and trust has grown between us. Trust is a unifying presence.

The four principles above are the foundation for the Living Write Tribe. Additional components include:

- Meals. We arrive in time for dinner on Friday and depart on Sunday at noon. Each member brings their own breakfast and lunch for Saturday plus Sunday morning breakfast. Dinners are a collaboration. We rotate the lead who prepares the main dish and identifies the other components for the rest of the meal. Members sign up for those items. We all bring snacks and bottled drinks and have far more than we need. Our time at the table is filled with laughter, and we share stories, experiences, and more.

- Feedback vs. Critique. Feedback is the lifeblood of improvement, essential to advancing your work. Several in the group had previous experience in critique groups which left them devastated. The process lacked balance, suggestions for improvement, and on occasion, kindness. To avoid this trustbuster, we do not do group critiques. A member may request feedback from the group at any time or contact an individual for feedback. We make ourselves available to one another between our retreats.

- We use *positive feedback* to ensure the individual knows what they did well and why it is valuable. *Developmental feedback* is used to assist the author in knowing what needs improvement, why that's important, and how to make the change. This approach keeps the focus on the work, not the individual.

ADDITIONAL PRACTICES AND PRINCIPLES

- Conferences. Members attend together whenever possible and gain a double blessing: information and the opportunity to deepen friendships. Nothing like sharing a room together to bring us closer!

- Friendship. We are all busy women, but our relationships have grown over the years. We are one another's cheerleaders and are quick to celebrate the successes of others. There is a true collaboration among the team. Competition is not in play.

If you'd like to connect with us via email, please feel free to do so at deb.dearmond@gmail.com

ENDNOTES

INTRODUCTION: AM I A WRITER?

1. Margery Williams, *Velveteen Rabbit* (Greg H. Doran Company, 1922), 19

2. Williams, *Velveteen Rabbit*, 19.

HUMBLE PIE DOES A BODY GOOD

1. *Everpedia*, s.v. "humility," accessed 27 Feb 2022, https://everipedia.org/Humility.

AND . . . IT'S A NO FROM ME

1. Emily Temple, "The Most-Rejected Books of all Time," *Literary Hub*, December 22, 2017, https://lithub.com/the-most-rejected-books-of-all-time/.

2. Hannah Preston, "'American Idol' Rejects: These Now Famous Musicians Were Turned Away by Judges," *Newsweek*, March 21, 2019, https://www.newsweek.com/american-idol-rejects-5-now-famous-musicians-who-were-not-put-through-1371733.

3. Peter Guralnick, *Last Train to Memphis: The Rise of Elvis Presley* (Boston: Little, Brown and Co., 1994), 29, 134, 426.

4. David Sheward, "7 Facts about Vincent van Gogh," *Biography*, updated June 17, 2020, https://www. biography.com/news/vincent-van-gogh-biography-facts.

TIGHTY WRITEY

1. *Lexico*, English dictionary, s.v. "edit," accessed February 27, 2022, https://www.lexico.com/en/definition/edit.

FOLLOW WHO?

1. *Blue Letter Bible*, Strong's Greek Lexicon (KJV), s.v. "deute," accessed 27 Feb 2022, https://www.blueletterbible.org/lexicon/g1205/kjv/tr/0-1/.

2. *Blue Letter Bible*, Strong's Greek Lexicon (KJV), s.v. "akoloutheō," accessed 27 Feb 2022, https://www.blueletterbible.org/lexicon/g190/kjv/tr/0-1/.

PARENT YOURSELF TO SUCCESS

1. *Dictionary*, s.v. "discipline," accessed 28 Feb 2022, https://www.dictionary.com/browse/disciple.

FIRST THINGS FIRST—PREPARE THE SOIL

1. Alexander Den Heijer, *Nothing You Don't Already Know: Remarkable Reminders about Meaning, Purpose, and Self-realization* (CreateSpace, May 17, 2018), n.p.

MAKE LIKE MARY

1. *Blue Letter Bible*, Strong's Greek Lexicon (ESV), s.v. "symballō," accessed 1 Mar 2022. https://www.blueletterbible.org/lexicon/g4820/esv/mgnt/0-1/.

CAT GOT YOUR TONGUE?

1. *Dictionary, s.v.* "normal," accessed 1 Mar 2022 https://www.dictionary.com/browse/normal.

WRITE? RIGHT!

1. Lorraine Santoli. "The Top Reason People Never Finish Writing Their Book." *Synergy Whisperer.* October 20, 2015, https://thesynergyexpert.com/2015/10/20/the-top-reason-people-never-finish-writing-their-book/#:~:text=Did%20you%20know%20that%2097%25%20of%20people%20who,do%20so%2C%20only%2030%20actually%20complete%20the%20task.

2. Jim Denney, "The Holy Call to Writing: Are You Called to Write?" *Inspire Christian Writers*, August 1, 2013, https://www.inspirewriters.com/the-holy-call-of-writing-are-you-called-to-write/.

PERFECTION AND PROCRASTINATION: PARTNERS IN CRIME

1. William Zinsser, *On Writing Well*, 30th Anniversary Edition (New York, NY: Collins, 2013), 24.

2. Dr. Timothy A. Pychyl, *Solving the Procrastination Puzzle: A Concise Guide to Strategies for Change* (TarcherPerigree, 2013), 40.

3. Pychyl, *Solving the Procrastination Puzzle.*

4. Pychyl, *Solving the Procrastination Puzzle.*

5. Zinsser, *Writing Well*, 20.